Workbook: Homework and Character Book
作業和寫字簿
to Accompany

Chinese Link
中 文 天 地

Zhōng   Wén   Tiān   Dì

Intermediate Chinese

Level 2	Part 2

吳素美   于月明   張燕輝
Sue-mei Wu   Yueming Yu   Yanhui Zhang

Carnegie Mellon University

PEARSON
Prentice Hall

world
Languages

Upper Saddle River, New Jersey 07458

Senior Acquisitions Editor: Rachel McCoy
Editorial Assistant: Alexei Soma
Director of Marketing: Kristine Suárez
Director of Editorial Development: Julia Caballero
Production Supervision: Nancy Stevenson
Project Manager: Margaret Chan, Graphicraft
Assistant Director of Production: Mary Rottino
Media Editor: Meriel Martínez
Senior Media Editor: Samantha Alducin
Prepress and Manufacturing Buyer: Christina Amato
Prepress and Manufacturing Assistant Manager: Mary Ann Gloriande
Senior Marketing Manager: Denise E. Miller
Marketing Coordinator: William J. Bliss
Publisher: Phil Miller
Cover Art Director: Jayne Conte
Cover Image: Richard Nowitz Photography

This book was set in 12/15 Sabon by Graphicraft Ltd., Hong Kong, and was printed
and bound by Bind-Rite Graphics, Inc. The cover was printed by Bind-Rite Graphics, Inc.

© 2008 by Pearson Education, Inc.
Upper Saddle River, NJ 07458

Printed in the United States of America
10 9 8 7 6 5 4 3 2 1

ISBN 0-13-613714-8
      978-0-13-613714-6

Pearson Education LTD., *London*
Pearson Education Australia PTY, Limited, *Sydney*
Pearson Education Singapore Pte. Ltd
Pearson Education North Asia Ltd., *Hong Kong*
Pearson Education Canada, Ltd., *Toronto*
Pearson Educación de México, S.A. de C.V.
Pearson Education-Japan, *Tokyo*
Pearson Education Malaysia, Pte. Ltd
Pearson Education, *Upper Saddle River*, New Jersey

目錄 (目录) CONTENTS

			Homework	Character Book

Character Book Indices

Lesson 15   I Have No Choice But to Ask for Your Help – Review
第十五課 我只好求你幫忙–復習
(第十五课 我只好求你帮忙–复习)

I. Listening exercises

A. Listen and then mark the correct statements with "✔" and incorrect ones with "✗":

New words:

躲(躲) [duǒ]: to hide

弄髒(弄脏) [nòngzāng]: to get dirty

灑(洒) [sǎ]: to spill

洗衣店(洗衣店) [xǐyīdiàn]: laundry

清洗(清洗) [qīngxǐ]: to clean

油跡(油迹) [yóujì]: oil stains

1. ( ) 麗麗這幾天一直在找學明。
   ( ) 丽丽这几天一直在找学明。

2. ( ) 學明是因為沒有給麗麗買到裙子，所以不敢見她。
   ( ) 学明是因为没有给丽丽买到裙子，所以不敢见她。

3. ( ) 學明是個粗心大意的人。
   ( ) 学明是个粗心大意的人。

4. ( ) 學明的衣服被弄髒了。
   ( ) 学明的衣服被弄脏了。

5. ( ) 麗麗和學明都不知道怎麼清洗衣服上的油跡。
   ( ) 丽丽和学明都不知道怎么清洗衣服上的油迹。

II. Character and vocabulary exercises

A. For each group of homographs, write down the Pinyin pronunciation, then make a sentence.

Example: 好：好不容易 [hǎo bù róngyì] 他好不容易給女朋友買到了磁帶。
好：好不容易 [hǎo bù róngyì] 他好不容易给女朋友买到了磁带。

        只好 [zhǐhǎo]   圖書館關門了，他只好回宿舍看書。
        只好 [zhǐhǎo]   图书馆关门了，他只好回宿舍看书。

        好客 [hàokè]   中國的少數民族大多數都很好客。
        好客 [hàokè]   中国的少数民族大多数都很好客。

        愛好者 [àihàozhě]   他是音樂愛好者。
        爱好者 [àihàozhě]   他是音乐爱好者。

1. 為：因為
   为：因为

       以為
       以为

       為了
       为了

2. 行：行不行
   行：行不行

       銀行
       银行

       流行
       流行

3. 地：地步
   地：地步

       好好地學
       好好地学

       地道
       地道

       地址
       地址

4. 倒：倒車
　　倒：倒车

　　　　倒楣
　　　　倒霉

5. 便：順便
　　便：顺便

　　　　便宜
　　　　便宜

　　　　方便
　　　　方便

6. 和：和好
　　和：和好

　　　　暖和
　　　　暖和

　　　　和你在一起
　　　　和你在一起

B. For each group of homophones, write down the Pinyin pronunciation and make a few sentences.

Example: [jìn] 進：上進　我的同學們都很上進。
　　　　　　 进：上进　我的同学们都很上进。

　　　　　　 近：很近　學校離宿舍很近。
　　　　　　 近：很近　学校离宿舍很近。

1. [　　] 件：
　　　　　件：

　　　　　見：
　　　　　见：

　　　　　健：
　　　　　健：

2. [   ] 段:

　　　　段:

　　　　鍛:

　　　　锻:

3. [   ] 近:

　　　　近:

　　　　進:

　　　　进:

4. [   ] 像:

　　　　像:

　　　　相:

　　　　相:

　　　　向:

　　　　向:

5. [   ] 中:

　　　　中:

　　　　終:

　　　　终:

　　　　鐘:

　　　　钟:

6. [   ] 再:

　　　　再:

　　　　在:

　　　　在:

　　　　載:

　　　　载:

C. Write the traditional forms for the following simplified characters, then write the pronunciation using Pinyin.

Example: 联络 __聯絡__ [liánluò]

                        Traditional Form   Pinyin

1. 发送 _____ _____

2. 录音机 _____ _____

3. 闹矛盾 _____ _____

4. 原谅 _____ _____

5. 保证 _____ _____

6. 购物 _____ _____

III. Grammar exercises

A. Read the passage and answer the following questions.

New words:

動物(动物) [dòngwù]: animal

微風(微风) [wēifēng]: gentle breeze

吹(吹) [chuī]: to blow

樹葉(树叶) [shùyè]: tree leaves

沙啦沙啦(沙啦沙啦) [shālā shālā]: (onomatopoeic expression) the sound of wind blowing through the trees

響(响) [xiǎng]: to make a sound

鳥(鸟) [niǎo]: bird

吱吱喳喳(吱吱喳喳) [zhīzhī zhāzhā]: (onomatopoeic expression) the chirping of birds

唱歌(唱歌) [chànggē]: to sing

遠處(远处) [yuǎnchù]: far away

傳(传) [chuán]: to pass

掉(掉) [diào]: to fall

槍(枪) [qiāng]: gun

打中(打中) [dǎzhòng]: to hit

群(群) [qún]: (measure word for groups)

佔領(占领) [zhànlǐng]: to occupy

打獵(打猎) [dǎliè]: to go hunting

砍(砍) [kǎn]: to chop; hack

草(草) [cǎo]: grass

枯(枯) [kū]: (of a plant) withered

花(花) [huā]: flower

謝(谢) [xiè]: to wilt, wither

根(根) [gēn]: root (of a plant)

樹椿(树桩) [shùzhuāng]: tree stump

孤零零(孤零零) [gūlínglíng]: solitary

站(站) [zhàn]: to stand

躲藏(躲藏) [duǒcáng]: to hide

火熱(火热) [huǒrè]: fervent

太陽(太阳) [tàiyáng]: the sun

照(照) [zhào]: to cast, shine

大地(大地) [dàdì]: earth; mother earth

溫度(温度) [wēndù]: temperature

忍受(忍受) [rěnshòu]: to bear; endure

紛紛(纷纷) [fēnfēn]: one after another

破壞(破坏) [pòhuài]: to destroy

開始(开始) [kāishǐ]: to begin

反思(反思) [fǎnsī]: to retrospect

植(植) [zhí]: to plant

種(种) [zhòng]: to plant

拯救(拯救) [zhěngjiù]: to save; rescue

樣子(样子) [yàngzi]: appearance

枝頭(枝头) [zhītóu]: tip of twig

愛護(爱护) [àihù]: to take good care of

地球(地球) [dìqiú]: the earth

永遠(永远) [yǒngyuǎn]: forever

記住(记住) [jìzhù]: to learn by heart

(繁體字)

　　在一個美麗的大森林裡，很多動物們都在那兒過著快樂的生活。一天，微風吹過，樹葉沙啦沙啦地響著，小鳥吱吱喳喳地唱著歌，天氣好極了。____ ____ (but) 正在這個時候，遠處傳來了"啪"的一聲，一隻小鳥從樹上掉了下來。原來它被槍打中了。

　　從這一天起，森林讓一群人給佔領了。他們有的打獵，有的砍樹，森林在短短的時間變了樣。小草枯了，花兒謝了，只有一根根樹樁孤零零地站著。動物們沒有家了，____ ____ (have to) 到處躲藏。這時候火熱的太陽照著大地，城市的溫度越來越高。人們忍受不了，紛紛來到森林。____ ____ (however) 他們走進去以後，____ (but) 不覺得涼快，還 ____ (even) 一隻動物____ 見不到。

　　看著被破壞的森林，人們開始反思，____ ____ (also) 開始植樹、種草，拯救被破壞了的森林。

　　一天一天過去了，森林回到了原來的樣子。小鳥在枝頭喳喳地唱著歌；小猴子在樹上撲通撲通地歡跳……

　　"愛護地球我們的家"，人們永遠記住了這句話。

(简体字)

　　在一个美丽的大森林里，很多动物们都在那儿过着快乐的生活。一天，微风吹过，树叶沙啦沙啦地响着，小鸟吱吱喳喳地唱着歌，天气好极了。____ ____ (but) 正在这个时候，远处传来了"啪"的一声，一只小鸟从树上掉了下来。原来它被枪打中了。

　　从这一天起，森林让一群人给占领了。他们有的打猎，有的砍树，森林在短短的时间变了样。小草枯了，花儿谢了，只有一根根树桩孤零零地站着。动物们没有家了，____ ____ (have to) 到处躲藏。这时候火热的太阳照着大地，城市的温度越来越高。人们忍受不了，纷纷来到森林。____ ____ (however) 他们走进去以后，____ (but) 不觉得凉快，还 ____ (even) 一只动物____ 见不到。

看着被破坏的森林，人们开始反思，____ ____ (also) 开始植树、种草，拯救被破坏了的森林。

一天一天过去了，森林回到了原来的样子。小鸟在枝头喳喳地唱着歌；小猴子在树上扑通扑通地欢跳......

"爱护地球我们的家"，人们永远记住了这句话。

1. With the help of English clues, fill in the blanks with appropriate conjunction words.
2. Underline sentences with subject or object omissions, then write the missing subject or object in the corresponding place.
3. Circle the markers of passive sentences, then re-write these sentences by using "把" structure.

_____

_____

_____

_____

IV. Media literacy reading exercises

(繁體字)

新手機　新享受

美華公司近日向全國推出了國內首款多媒體手機，這款手機將數碼相機、MP3及MP4播放器整合於一體，並與傳統家電互聯互通，提供消費者一個絕佳享受和時尚娛樂的新生活。

(简体字)

新手机　新享受

　　美华公司近日向全国推出了国内首款多媒体手机，这款手机将数码相机、MP3及MP4播放器整合于一体，并与传统家电互联互通，提供消费者一个绝佳享受和时尚娱乐的新生活。

Useful words and expressions:

享受(享受) [xiǎngshòu]: to enjoy; enjoyment

推出(推出) [tuīchū]: to introduce (a new product)

首款(首款) [shǒukuǎn]: the very first style

多媒體(多媒体) [duōméitǐ]: multimedia

將……整合於一體(将……整合于一体) [jiāng . . . zhěnghéyu yìtǐ]: to combine . . .
　　as one

播放器(播放器) [bōfàngqì]: audio visual player

並(并) [bìng]: moreover

與(与) [yǔ]: together with

傳統家電(传统家电) [chuántǒng jiādiàn]: traditional electrical appliances for families

互聯互通(互联互通) [hù lián hù tōng]: to be (all) connected

消費者(消费者) [xiāofèizhě]: consumer

絕佳享受(绝佳享受) [juéjiā xiǎngshòu]: extremely good enjoyment

時尚娛樂(时尚娱乐) [shíshàng yúlè]: entertainment activities in vogue

问题(问题):

1. Translate the headlines into English.

_____

2. Translate the passage into English.

_____

_____

_____

_____

_____

_____

3. Please find at least five written form expressions and give their equivalent spoken forms. [e.g. 近日(近日), 與(与) . . . etc.]

_____

V. Comprehensive exercises

我被誤會了(我被误会了)

Please write your experience of how you were misunderstood, and how you clarified yourself in the end. Try to use passive constructions, organize the essay with appropriate conjunction words, and apply adequate subject/object patterns. (At least 15 sentences)

_____

_____

_____

_____

_____

_____

Lesson 16　We Must Come to Visit You
第十六課　我們非過來看您不可
(第十六课　我们非过来看您不可)

I. Listening exercises

A. Listen and then mark the correct statements with "✔" and incorrect ones with "✗":

New words:

賀卡(贺卡) [hèkǎ]: greeting card

郵局(邮局) [yóujú]: post office

省(省) [shěng]: to economize; save

努力(努力) [nǔlì]: to make efforts

年輕有為(年轻有为) [niánqīng yǒuwéi]: young and having outstanding achievements

1. (　) 美玲正在給一個同學寫信。
   (　) 美玲正在给一个同学写信。

2. (　) 美玲的同學們都已經畢業了，現在都在努力地工作著。
   (　) 美玲的同学们都已经毕业了，现在都在努力地工作着。

3. (　) 建明還在電腦公司打工。
   (　) 建明还在电脑公司打工。

4. (　) 正平還沒有畢業。
   (　) 正平还没有毕业。

5. (　) 正平和他的女朋友都在加州 ([Jiāzhōu]: California)。
   (　) 正平和他的女朋友都在加州。

II. Character exercises

A. For each group of homographs, write down the Pinyin pronunciation, then make a sentence.

Example: 當：當教授 [dāng jiàoshòu] 小麗的理想是當一個教授。
　　　　 当：当教授 [dāng jiàoshòu] 小丽的理想是当一个教授。

當成 [dàngchéng]	這些小朋友們把老師當成媽媽了。
当成 [dàngchéng]	这些小朋友们把老师当成妈妈了。
當然 [dāngrán]	我媽媽包的餃子當然好吃。
当然 [dāngrán]	我妈妈包的饺子当然好吃。
當天 [dāngtiān]	小明當天就把功課做完了。
当天 [dāngtiān]	小明当天就把功课做完了。

1. 教：教書
   教：教书

   教練
   教练

   教中文
   教中文

2. 應：應用
   应：应用

   應該
   应该

3. 過：去過中國
   过：去过中国

   過獎
   过奖

   過生日
   过生日

4. 處：待人處世
   处：待人处世

   到處
   到处

B. For each group of homophones, create phases and make a few sentences.

Example: [liú] 留：留學　小王畢業以後去英國留學了。
　　　　　　留：留学　小王毕业以后去英国留学了。

流：流行　我喜歡聽流行音樂。
流：流行　我喜欢听流行音乐。

1. [　　] 道：
　　　　道：

　　　　倒：
　　　　倒：

　　　　到：
　　　　到：

2. [　　] 待：
　　　　待：

　　　　代：
　　　　代：

　　　　帶：
　　　　帶：

3. [　　] 其：
　　　　其：

　　　　齊：
　　　　齐：

　　　　騎：
　　　　骑：

4. [　　] 寄：
　　　　寄：

　　　　繼：
　　　　继：

　　　　濟：
　　　　济：

　　　　記：
　　　　记：

5. [　] 想：

想：

響：

响：

6. [　] 趁：

趁：

襯：

衬：

7. [　] 續：

续：

蓄：

蓄：

8. [　] 落：

落：

絡：

络：

C. Write the traditional forms for the following simplified characters, then write the pronunciation using Pinyin.

Example: 继续 ___繼續___ [jìxù]

Traditional Form	Pinyin
1. 宝贵 _____	_____
2. 过奖 _____	_____
3. 专心 _____	_____
4. 经验 _____	_____
5. 看齐 _____	_____
6. 打扰 _____	_____

III. Grammar exercises

● **A.** Read the passage and answer the following questions.

New words:

窮人(穷人) [qióngrén]: poor people

嘆一口氣(叹一口气) [tànyìkǒuqì]: to sigh for one breath

聞(闻) [wén]: to smell

香味(香味) [xiāngwèi]: sweet smell; scent

告(告) [gào]: to accuse

法官(法官) [fǎguān]: judge

公道(公道) [gōngdào]: justice

答應(答应) [dāying]: to agree; promise

教訓(教训) [jiàoxun]: to give somebody a lesson

行禮(行礼) [xínglǐ]: to salute

裝(装) [zhuāng]: to hold

硬幣(硬币) [yìngbì]: coin

袋子(袋子) [dàizi]: bag

搖(摇) [yáo]: to shake; wave

●

大搖大擺(大摇大摆) [dàyáo dàbǎi]: to swagger; to walk haughtily

(繁體字)

　　有一天，一個窮人來找高明，說："高明，我想求你一件事，你 ____ ____ ____ (have to) 幫我呀！"

　　"沒問題，我 ____ ____ ____ (will definitely) 幫你的，有什麼事你就說吧。"高明說。窮人嘆了一口氣說："昨天我在飯館門前坐著休息了一會兒，這家飯館老闆就出來說我聞了他的飯菜的香味，____ (have to) 讓我給飯錢 ____ ____。我當然不給，於是老闆就告了我。我今天就要見法官了。你能去幫我說幾句公道話嗎？"

　　高明一口答應下來，說："行！我 ____ (must) 幫你教訓一下這個

● 老闆 ____ ____ 。"他馬上就和那個窮人一起去見法官。到了法官那兒，高明對法官行了個禮，說："這個人是我大哥。他沒有錢，飯錢由我

付給飯館老闆好了。"高明說著拿出一個裝硬幣的小袋子。他搖了搖袋子，問飯館老闆："你聽到我的錢在響嗎？"

"我聽到了，聽到了。"老闆高興地說。

"好了，老闆，他聞了你飯菜的香味，你聽了我的錢的響聲，這件事 ____ (then) 就完了。"說完，高明就拉著那個窮人的手，大搖大擺地走了。

(简体字)

有一天，一个穷人来找高明，说："高明，我想求你一件事，你 ____ ____ ____ (have to) 帮我呀！"

"没问题，我 ____ ____ ____ (will definitely) 帮你的，有什么事你就说吧。"高明说。穷人叹了一口气说："昨天我在饭馆门前坐着休息了一会儿，这家饭馆老板就出来说我闻了他的饭菜的香味，____ (have to) 让我给饭钱 ____ ____。我当然不给，于是老板就告了我。我今天就要见法官了。你能去帮我说几句公道话吗？"

高明一口答应下来，说："行！我 ____ (must) 帮你教训一下这个老板 ____ ____。"他马上就和那个穷人一起去见法官。到了法官那儿，高明对法官行了个礼，说："这个人是我大哥。他没有钱，饭钱由我付给饭馆老板好了。"高明说着拿出一个装硬币的小袋子。他摇了摇袋子，问饭馆老板："你听到我的钱在响吗？"

"我听到了，听到了。"老板高兴地说。

"好了，老板，他闻了你饭菜的香味，你听了我的钱的响声，这件事 ____ (then) 就完了。"说完，高明就拉着那个穷人的手，大摇大摆地走了。

1. With the help of English clues, fill in the blanks with appropriate words that emphasize the tones the sentences.

2. Underline and identify the semantic relationship of serial verb constructions in the text. Write down the semantic meaning on top of the corresponding sentence in the text. Then summarize which semantic relationship is mostly used in the verb construction in stories.

(I) Sequence   (II) Purpose   (III) Alternating

(IV) Circumstance   (V) Instrument or vehicle   (VI) Accompanying circumstances

_____

_____

_____

B. Translation:

New words:

校慶(校庆) [xiàoqìng]: anniversary of the founding of a school or college

校友(校友) [xiàoyǒu]: alumni

微笑(微笑) [wēixiào]: smile

重聚(重聚) [chóngjù]: gather together again

招牌菜(招牌菜) [zhāopáicài]: signature dish

大人(大人) [dàren]: adult; grown-up

遊戲(游戏) [yóuxì]: game; play

友誼(友谊) [yǒuyì]: friendship

發展(发展) [fāzhǎn]: to develop; expand

下一代(下一代) [xiàyídài]: next generation

1. _____

   (March 15 is the 100-year anniversary of the founding of Xiaoming's university.)

2. _____

   (On that day, the campus was packed with alumni from all over the places.)

3. _____

   (Smiles are hanging on their faces.)

4. _____

   _____

(Taking this opportunity, Xiaoming and his classmates made an appointment to gather together at the university.)

5. _____

   _____

(What's more, they are going to dine together at their favorite restaurant from their university years.)

6. _____

(Although they had graduated ten years ago, the restaurant has remained the same.)

7. _____

(The boss is the same boss. Even the signature dishes are the same.)

8. _____

   _____

(The classmates haven't met for five years. They had endless things to talk about after meeting each other.)

9. _____

(Some even brought their children with them.)

10. _____

    _____

(Then while the adults were smiling and chatting together, the children were yielding and playing games together.)

11. _____

    _____

(All the classmates said that they had to continue their friendship to the next generation.)

IV. Media literacy reading exercises

(繁體字)

> # 苦練9年　83歲翁開書法展
>
> 　　83歲老人周先生，九年前右手食指因公受傷截了一段，又痛又麻。他靠著寫毛筆字，治癒手指痛，寫得一手好字，也練就強而有力的手勁。昨天起至二十五日在活動中心舉辦書法個展，與親友分享他的書法心得。

(简体字)

> # 苦练9年　83岁翁开书法展
>
> 　　83岁老人周先生，九年前右手食指因公受伤截了一段，又痛又麻。他靠着写毛笔字，治愈手指痛，写得一手好字，也练就强而有力的手劲。昨天起至二十五日在活动中心举办书法个展，与亲友分享他的书法心得。

Useful words and expressions:

苦練(苦练) [kǔliàn]: to practice very hard at

翁(翁) [wēng]: old man

書法展(书法展) [shūfǎzhǎn]: calligraphy exhibition

因公受傷(因公受伤) [yīn gōng shòushāng]: to be injured while at work

又痛又麻(又痛又麻) [yòu tòng yòu má]: (to be) painful and numb

靠(靠) [kào]: by (doing something)

毛筆字(毛笔字) [máobǐzì]: calligraphy

治癒(治愈) [zhìyù]: to cure

寫得一手好字(写得一手好字) [xiěde yìshǒu hǎozì]: to be able to do very good handwriting

練就(练就) [liànjiù]: to succeed in . . . through practice

強而有力(强而有力) [qiáng'éryǒulì]: strong and powerful

手勁(手劲) [shǒujìn]: strength of the hand

活動中心(活动中心) [huódòngzhōngxīn]: activity center

舉辦(举办) [jǔbàn]: to hold and sponsor

個展(个展) [gèzhǎn]: exhibition of one's own works

與(与) [yǔ]: together with

親友(亲友) [qīnyǒu]: relatives and friends

分享......心得(分享......心得) [fēnxiǎng xīndé]: to share one's own thoughts on . . .

問題(问题):

1. Translate the headlines into English.

   _____

2. What problem did 周先生 have with his finger?

   _____

3. What has he achieved through calligraphy practice?

   _____

4. What is a 書法個展(书法个展)? Why did 周先生 do it?

   _____

5. Find at least three written form expressions in this short paragraph and give their equivalent oral forms.

   _____

   _____

V. Comprehensive exercises

同學們都想來看您(同学们都想来看您)

Writing: Several of your best friends from high school plan to have a gathering and then visit your teacher's house. As you are the coordinator of this gathering, please send an email to your teacher, telling him/her about your friends' current situation now and inquire of your teacher what would be the best time to visit him/her.
(At least 15 sentences)

_____

_____

_____

_____

_____

_____

_____

_____

_____

_____

Lesson 17   Didn't You Apply for an Internship Last Year?
第十七課 你難道不是去年申請實習了嗎?
(第十七课 你难道不是去年申请实习了吗?)

I. Listening exercises

張秋英今年夏天要去一家公司實習。她的室友小紅明年也要申請實習了。今天他們倆在宿舍裡聊天 ([liáotiān]: to chat)。秋英在給小紅介紹她的申請經驗:

张秋英今年夏天要去一家公司实习。她的室友小红明年也要申请实习了。今天他们俩在宿舍里聊天。秋英在给小红介绍她的申请经验:

A. In each box below, mark "✔" if the statement is correct, "✗" if it is wrong:

1. (　) 秋英明年就要申請實習了，所以她很擔心。
   (　) 秋英明年就要申请实习了，所以她很担心。

2. (　) 秋英又聰明又能幹，條件非常好。
   (　) 秋英又聪明又能干，条件非常好。

3. (　) 寫簡歷的時候，要把自己的能力和最好的條件寫清楚。
   (　) 写简历的时候，要把自己的能力和最好的条件写清楚。

4. (　) 網上的信息太多，太花時間，所以不要在網上申請。
   (　) 网上的信息太多，太花时间，所以不要在网上申请。

5. (　) 申請工作很複雜，又難又花時間。
   (　) 申请工作很复杂，又难又花时间。

B. Answer the following questions based on what you have heard from the dialogue:

1. 秋英有沒有找到實習的工作? 為什麼前幾天她一直在擔心?
   秋英有没有找到实习的工作? 为什么前几天她一直在担心?

   _____ 。

2. 寫簡歷的時候，首先一定要做什麼？
   写简历的时候，首先一定要做什么？

   _____。

3. 寫好簡歷以後，下一步要做什麼？
   写好简历以后，下一步要做什么？

   _____。

4. 在招聘網站上還可以做什麼？
   在招聘网站上还可以做什么？

   _____。

5. 請教授寫推薦信的時候，一定要注意什麼？
   请教授写推荐信的时候，一定要注意什么？

   _____。

II. Character and vocabulary exercises

A. Write out the Pinyin and make a phrase for each of the following homophones. Then use the phrase to make a sentence:

	Pinyin	Phrase	Sentence
1. ( ) 記		_____	_____
记		_____	_____
計		_____	_____
计		_____	_____
寄		_____	_____
寄		_____	_____

績 _____ _____

绩 _____ _____

2. ( ) 句 _____ _____

句 _____ _____

拒 _____ _____

拒 _____ _____

劇 _____ _____

剧 _____ _____

據 _____ _____

据 _____ _____

B. Please use the expressions provided to complete the following conversation. You may use an expression twice if necessary:

哪兒啊(哪儿啊)，說說看(说说看)，首先(首先)，那就是說(那就是说)，
擔心(担心)，正是如此(正是如此)，條件(条件)，拒絕(拒绝)，
下一步(下一步)，但願如此(但愿如此)，能幹(能干)，
對.....感興趣(对.....感兴趣)

(繁體字)

A. 還有一個學期我們就要畢業了，你一定找到工作了吧?

B. _____! 我還沒有開始申請呢。

A. 是嗎? 我已經找到工作了。

B. _____，你現在不用擔心了。來，_____，你是怎麼申請的?

A. _____，我把簡歷寫好，_____ 我從網上下載申請表格，填好了以後發出去，我還找了幾位教授給我寫推薦信。_____ 就是等公司的消息了。

B. 你申請了幾家公司?

A. 八家，我被五家公司 _____ 了。

B. _____ 有三家公司對你 _____。是嗎?

A. _____。

B. 我也就是怕被公司 _____。

A. 其實你不用 _____，你很 _____，_____ 很好。你一定會找到工作的。

B. _____。

(简体字)

A. 还有一个学期我们就要毕业了，你一定找到工作了吧?

B. _____! 我还没有开始申请呢。

A. 是吗? 我已经找到工作了。

B. _____，你现在不用担心了。来，_____，你是怎么申请的?

A. _____，我把简历写好，_____ 我从网上下载申请表格，填好了以后发出去，我还找了几位教授给我写推荐信。_____ 就是等公司的消息了。

B. 你申请了几家公司?

A. 八家，我被五家公司 _____ 了。

B. _____ 有三家公司对你 _____。是吗？

A. _____ 。

B. 我也就是怕被公司 _____ 。

A. 其实你不用 _____，你很 _____，_____ 很好。你一定会找

　　到工作的。

B. _____ 。

III. Grammar exercises

A. Based on the following situations, ask rhetorical questions with " 不是……嗎?
(不是……吗?)", " 沒有……嗎?(没有……吗?)" to confirm what you know
or elicit more information:

1. 我的朋友說要買一個數碼相機。
   我的朋友说要买一个数码相机。
   _____

2. 我的肚子疼。
   我的肚子疼。
   _____

3. 我跟女朋友吵架了。
   我跟女朋友吵架了。
   _____

4. 建明說他開了一家小小的電腦公司。
   建明说他开了一家小小的电脑公司。
   _____

B. The following information is not given in the right order. Please rearrange them in the right order using the appropriate procedural words to make sentences:

Words and expressions indicating procedures:

首先
第一
第一步

1. Making a travel plan:

   找住的地方(找住的地方)，租車(租车)，決定去哪兒旅遊(决定去哪儿旅游)，開車出去(开车出去)，從網上下載地圖(从网上下载地图)

   _____

   _____

   _____

   _____ 。

2. To apply for a graduate program:

   把表填好(把表填好)，決定申請哪個學校(决定申请哪个学校)，把表寄出去(把表寄出去)，從網上下載申請表(从网上下载申请表)，在網上查學校的網站(在网上查学校的网站)

   _____

   _____

   _____

   _____ 。

IV. Media literacy reading exercises

The following is the resumé of a student in China. Read it with the help of a dictionary and answer the questions below:

(繁體字)

史小華

  通信地址: 上海市南京街10號   郵政編碼: 567890

  電話號碼: (021)987654321   手機號碼: 00135-12345

  電子郵件: xiaohua@zhongwen.edu

技能總結

英語水平:

  通過國家英語四級考試。能熟練地聽、說、讀、寫。能熟練運用網絡查閱並翻譯英文資料。

計算機水平:

  通過國家二級考試,熟悉網絡和電子商務。

實習經歷

  2006年7–8月在上海電子商務網站實習。主要工作是

1. 在網絡上查國內以及國外的商務。 2. 搜集、整理中英文資料。

3. 翻譯英文資料。

教育背景

  2003年9月——2007年7月上海大學企業管理(本科)

  2000年9月——2003年7月上海市第一中學

主修課程: 數學、計算機管理、電子商務、市場開發、西方經濟學、
        國際貿易

獲獎情況: 兩次獲學校獎學金

史小华

通信地址：上海市南京街10号　　邮政编码：567890

电话号码：(021)987654321　　　手机号码：00135-12345

电子邮件：xiaohua@zhongwen.edu

技能总结

英语水平：

通过国家英语四级考试。能熟练地听、说、读、写。能熟练运用网络查阅并翻译英文资料。

计算机水平：

通过国家二级考试，熟悉网络和电子商务。

实习经历

2006年7-8月在上海电子商务网站实习。主要工作是

1. 在网络上查国内以及国外的商务。2. 搜集、整理中英文资料。

3. 翻译英文资料。

教育背景

2003年9月——2007年7月上海大学企业管理(本科)

2000年9月——2003年7月上海市第一中学

主修课程：数学、计算机管理、电子商务、市场开发、西方经济学、国际贸易

获奖情况：两次获学校奖学金

Useful words and expressions:

通信地址(通信地址) [tōngxìn dìzhǐ]: mailing address

郵政編碼(邮政编码) [yóuzhèng biānmǎ]: zip code

技能(技能) [jìnéng]: skills, techniques

總結(总结) [zǒngjié]: summary

水平(水平) [shuǐpíng]: level

通過(通过) [tōngguò]: to pass

級(级) [jí]: grade

熟練(熟练) [shúliàn]: skillful

運用(运用) [yùnyòng]: to use

網絡(网络) [wǎngluò]: the Internet

查閱(查阅) [cháyuè]: to consult, check

翻譯(翻译) [fānyì]: to translate

資料(资料) [zīliào]: material

熟悉(熟悉) [shúxī]: to be familiar with

商務(商务) [shāngwù]: business

經歷(经历) [jīnglì]: experience

資訊(资讯) [zīxùn]: information

搜集(搜集) [sōují]: to collect, gather

整理(整理) [zhěnglǐ]: to clean up

教育背景(教育背景) [jiàoyù bèijǐng]: educational background

企業管理(企业管理) [qǐyè guǎnlǐ]: business administration

本科(本科) [běnkē]: undergraduate

主修(主修) [zhǔxiū]: (academic) major

市場開發(市场开发) [shìchǎng kāifā]: marketing

西方經濟學(西方经济学) [xīfāng jīngjìxué]: western economy

國際貿易(国际贸易) [guójì màoyì]: international trade

獲獎情況(获奖情况) [huòjiǎng qíngkuàng]: award information

獎學金(奖学金) [jiǎngxuéjīn]: scholarship

問題(问题):

1. What is her major? What kind of a job is she looking for?

_____

2. What major skills does she have?

_____

3. Has she had any internship experience? If so, where?

_____

V. Comprehensive exercises

Take the resumé above as an example and, write your own resumé. Your resumé should include (but not be limited to) the following points,

1. Your major
2. Your education
3. Your Chinese language proficiency
4. Your internship experience
5. Activities you have participated in school
6. Your hobby

_____

_____

_____

_____

_____

_____

_____

_____

Lesson 18   The Company Has Around 300 Employees
第十八課 公司的員工有三百個左右
(第十八课 公司的员工有三百个左右)

I. Listening exercises

Your girl friend 小琴(小琴) is on the telephone being interviewed by a job recruiter. The recruiter wants to know why she thinks she is qualified for the job they have advertised. Listen to what she says and then answer the following questions:

1. 小琴的大學專業是 (小琴的大学专业是)

　　a. 計算機科學 (计算机科学)

　　b. 商學 (商学)

　　c. 計算機和商學 (计算机和商学)

2. 只要有機會, 小琴 (只要有机会, 小琴)

　　a. 成績就是A (成绩就是A)

　　b. 就參加新年的活動 (就参加新年的活动)

　　c. 就組織一些活動 (就组织一些活动)

3. 小琴組織的新年活動 (小琴组织的新年活动)

　　a. 參加的人很多, 大概有五百個人左右
　　　 (参加的人很多, 大概有五百个人左右)

　　b. 因為太花時間, 所以影響了她的學習
　　　 (因为太花时间, 所以影响了她的学习)

　　c. 由於太花時間, 因此沒有很多人參加
　　　 (由于太花时间, 因此没有很多人参加)

4. 除了學習以外, 小琴還 (除了学习以外, 小琴还)

　　a. 常常去公司實習 (常常去公司实习)

　　b. 常常受到公司的嘉獎 (常常受到公司的嘉奖)

　　c. 在公司實習了三個月左右 (在公司实习了三个月左右)

II. Character and vocabulary exercises

A. Each of the following characters can be used to form different words and phrases. Based on what you have learned, write at least two phrases for each character.

1. 機 _____ _____ _____ _____ _____
   机 _____ _____ _____ _____ _____

2. 務 _____ _____ _____ _____ _____
   务 _____ _____ _____ _____ _____

3. 從 _____ _____ _____ _____ _____
   从 _____ _____ _____ _____ _____

4. 開 _____ _____ _____ _____ _____
   开 _____ _____ _____ _____ _____

5. 發 _____ _____ _____ _____ _____
   发 _____ _____ _____ _____ _____

B. Make sentences with the following expressions:

1. 對......感興趣(对......感兴趣)

   _____

2. 提供(提供)

   _____

3. 多次(多次)

   _____

4. 除了......以外(除了......以外)

   _____

5. 凡是(凡是)

   _____

III. Grammar exercises

A. Complete the following complex sentences based on the clues given:

1. 我的女朋友不但_____ (has high scores), 而且
_____ (she has strong leadership ability as well)。

   我的女朋友不但_____ (has high scores), 而且
_____ (she has strong leadership ability as well)。

2. 儘管 _____ (our company does not have a long history),
但是我們公司發展得很快。

   尽管 _____ (our company does not have a long history),
但是我们公司发展得很快。

3. 我爸爸是做計算機工作的, 因此 _____
(he is interested in many new software technologies)。

   我爸爸是做计算机工作的, 因此 _____
(he is interested in many new software technologies)。

4. 要是 _____ (want to apply to graduate school),
你就應該去查大學研究院的網站。

   要是 _____ (want to apply to graduate school),
你就应该去查大学研究院的网站。

5. 無論 _____ (what job you assign to her), 她都會很努力
地去做。

   无论 _____ (what job you assign to her), 她都会很努力
地去做。

B. Answer the following questions with words indicating approximation:

1. 請說說看，你們大學有多少個專業？
   请说说看，你们大学有多少个专业？

   _____

2. 你知道通用電氣公司(GE)有多少員工？
   你知道通用电气公司(GE)有多少员工？

   _____

3. 你能告訴我你有多少光碟嗎？
   你能告诉我你有多少光碟吗？

   _____

IV. Media literacy reading exercises

(繁體字)

廣州萬餘職位迎聘 "海歸"

　　第七屆中國留學人員廣州科技交流會將於12月28日至30日舉行。據介紹，全國進入 "211工程" 的50多所高校、廣州人事局、全國留學服務中心等單位將提供上萬個職位到 "留交會" 進行招聘。

(简体字)

广州万余职位迎聘 "海归"

　　第七届中国留学人员广州科技交流会将于12月28日至30日举行。据介绍，全国进入 "211工程" 的50多所高校、广州人事局、全国留学服务中心等单位将提供上万个职位到 "留交会" 进行招聘。

Useful words and expressions:

廣州(广州) [Guǎngzhōu]: Guangzhou, a major city in south China

萬(万) [wàn]: ten thousand

餘(余) [yú]: over

職位(职位) [zhíwèi]: position

海歸(海归) [hǎiguī]: abbreviation of "海外歸來(的人)[海外归来(的人)]" referring to people who have studied or worked abroad but have now returned to China

留學人員(留学人员) [liúxué rényuán]: people who study abroad

科技交流會(科技交流会) [kējì jiāoliúhuì]: science and technology communication meeting

舉行(举行) [jǔxíng]: to hold

211工程: A government project in the year 1999 which involved 100 universities in China. The number 21 refers to the 21st century, and 1 refers to 100 universities. It aimed at helping 100 universities in China become first-rate universities to meet the challenges of the 21st century.

高校(高校) [gāoxiào]: college or university

人事局(人事局) [rénshìjú]: human resource bureau

單位(单位) [dānwèi]: work units

留交會(留交会) [liújiāohuì]: abbreviation of 留學人員科技交流會(留学人员科技交流会)

問題(问题):

1. Translate the headlines into English.

   _____

2. How many times has this kind of "留交會(留交会)" been held so far?

   _____

3. In total, how many positions are provided to people who have returned to China from abroad?

   _____

4. Who has provided the positions?

   _____

V. Comprehensive exercises

Suppose you are now job hunting. Write a statement (at least 250 words) to introduce yourself to hiring companies. Try to make yourself as competitive as possible.

_____

_____

_____

_____

_____

_____

_____

_____

_____

Lesson 19   I Would Rather Go to the Financial Bank
第十九課 我倒寧願去金融銀行
(第十九课 我倒宁愿去金融银行)

I. Listening exercises

A. 大中(大中) has worked in a bank for two years. Today he's back to visit his friends who are still studying at the university. They are graduating soon and are looking for jobs. They need more information and suggestions. 大中(大中) is now telling them how he feels about his job and what suggestions he has for them. Listen to what he says and then answer the questions below:

New words:

平時(平时) [píngshí]: usually

怪(怪) [guài]: to complain

1. Decide whether the following statements are true or false. Mark a "✔" in the box given if the statement is true and put an "✗" if it is false:

a. ( ) 因為大中在銀行的工作太忙了，所以他一年都沒有去看
他的朋友們。
( ) 因为大中在银行的工作太忙了，所以他一年都没有去看
他的朋友们。

b. ( ) 大中覺得他的工作太忙不好。
( ) 大中觉得他的工作太忙不好。

c. ( ) 大中常常擔心他的工作。
( ) 大中常常担心他的工作。

d. ( ) 大中和同事之間的關係很融洽。
( ) 大中和同事之间的关系很融洽。

e. ( ) 大中覺得常常要出差很幸運。
( ) 大中觉得常常要出差很幸运。

f. ( ) 銀行的工資不高，福利待遇也不太好。
( ) 银行的工资不高，福利待遇也不太好。

g. ( ) 大中不能去上研究生院的課，因為他要在工作三年以後才有學費補貼。

( ) 大中不能去上研究生院的课，因为他要在工作三年以后才有学费补贴。

h. ( ) 大中覺得工資固然重要，可是福利待遇和工作環境更重要。

( ) 大中觉得工资固然重要，可是福利待遇和工作环境更重要。

B. Listen to the tape again and write out at least FIVE positive things about 大中's job at the bank:

a. _____

b. _____

c. _____

d. _____

e. _____

II. Character and vocabulary exercises

A. Circle all the simplified characters in the following paragraph and write them in the traditional form:

这几年经济情况不太好，就业市场不景气，找工作不容易。我很幸运，已经找到工作了，去一家计算机软件开发公司工作。虽然他们付的工资不算太高，可是福利待遇还不错，医疗保险很好。这是最重要的。我去面试的时候见到了很多同事。看上去他们之间的关系不错。我希望那儿的工作环境很好，这样我就可以好好地工作了。

_____

_____

_____

_____

_____

B. Select the right character and fill in the blanks in the following sentences:

道(道)，經(经)，修(修)，資(资)，慮(虑)，競(竞)，屬(厉)，休(休)，
遇(遇)，境(境)，輕(轻)，虛(虚)，歷(历)，咨(咨)

a. 我現在正在考＿＿＿ 找工作。

我现在正在考 ＿＿＿ 找工作。

新民是一個很謙 ＿＿＿ 的人。

新民是一个很谦 ＿＿＿ 的人。

b. 昨天我把簡＿＿＿ 發出去了。

昨天我把简 ＿＿＿ 发出去了。

她很 ＿＿＿害，已經找到工作了。

她很 ＿＿＿害，已经找到工作了。

c. 現在＿＿＿ 濟還沒有完全恢復。

现在 ＿＿＿ 济还没有完全恢复。

年＿＿＿人總是會有機會的。

年＿＿＿人总是会有机会的。

d. 我的工作待＿＿＿ 不錯。

我的工作待 ＿＿＿ 不错。

他說的話有＿＿＿ 理。

他说的话有＿＿＿ 理。

e. 就業市場＿＿＿ 爭很屬害。

就业市场 ＿＿＿ 争很厉害。

這兒的工作環＿＿＿很好。

这儿的工作环＿＿＿很好。

f. 你爸爸退＿＿＿了嗎?

你爸爸退＿＿＿了吗?

這個學期你＿＿＿了多少課?

这个学期你＿＿＿了多少课?

g. 這個公司給的工＿＿＿不太高。

这个公司给的工＿＿＿不太高。

你想去一個＿＿＿詢公司工作嗎?

你想去一个＿＿＿询公司工作吗?

III. Grammar exercises

A. 小金(小金) and 小周(小周) will be juniors next semester. Now they are chatting in the dorm about their future. Use the following expressions to complete the dialogue between them. You may use them repeatedly if necessary:

倒(倒)，固然(固然)，卻(却)，到底(到底)，非......不可(非......不可)

金: 小周，你說，我們現在考慮畢業以後的工作是不是太早了?

金: 小周，你说，我们现在考虑毕业以后的工作是不是太早了?

周: 我＿＿＿覺得我們應該考慮了。

周: 我＿＿＿觉得我们应该考虑了。

金: 畢業以後你想不想馬上工作?

金: 毕业以后你想不想马上工作?

周：能找一個好的工作 ____ 不錯，可是我也非常想去讀研究生院。
我覺得要想以後在就業市場上有競爭力，就 ____ 多學習一些知
識 ____ 。

周：能找一个好的工作 ____ 不错，可是我也非常想去读研究生院。
我觉得要想以后在就业市场上有竞争力，就 ____ 多学习一些知
识 ____ 。

金：我 ____ 不太同意你的想法。你想，你學了很多知識， ____ 沒有
實際 [shíjì] (practical) 的工作能力，那有什麼用啊！我 ____ 是覺得
先工作，以後再去讀研究生院比較好。

金：我 ____ 不太同意你的想法。你想，你学了很多知识， ____ 没有
实际的工作能力，那有什么用啊！我 ____ 是觉得先工作，以后
再去读研究生院比较好。

周：你 ____ 覺得知識 ([zhīshi]: knowledge) 重要還是工作經驗重要？
周：你 ____ 觉得知识重要还是工作经验重要？

金：我覺得兩個都重要。要有競爭力 ____ 要有實際工作經驗 ____ 。
金：我觉得两个都重要。要有竞争力 ____ 要有实际工作经验 ____ 。

周：工作經驗 ____ 重要，但是我們現在還年輕，應該在學校裡多學
一些東西。我爸爸也是這麼跟我說的。

周：工作经验 ____ 重要，但是我们现在还年轻，应该在学校里多学
一些东西。我爸爸也是这么跟我说的。

金：你爸爸的話＿＿＿有道理，不過我還是想先工作。

金：你爸爸的话＿＿＿有道理，不过我还是想先工作。

周：我可能也會先找工作。不過我是一定要讀研究生院的。

周：我可能也会先找工作。不过我是一定要读研究生院的。

B. Provide a suggestion regarding your friend's concern by using the conjunctions provided:

1. 我想找他幫忙，可是我不太了解他。 （如果……就）
   我想找他帮忙，可是我不太了解他。 （如果……就）

   _____

2. 我想去看電影，可是還沒有準備好明天的考試。 （只有……才）
   我想去看电影，可是还没有准备好明天的考试。 （只有……才）

   _____

3. 你說我最應該考慮哪個好呢，錢還是工作環境呢？ （固然……可是）
   你说我最应该考虑哪个好呢，钱还是工作环境呢？ （固然……可是）

   _____

IV. Media literacy reading exercises

Read the following news with the help of a dictionary and answer the questions below:

(繁體字)

人事部服務中心為海歸提供推薦服務

　　國家人事部留學人員和專家服務中心已開展"海外留學人員回國工作或創業推薦"業務。希望回國工作或創業的海外留學人員可及時聯繫該服務處。

(简体字)

人事部服务中心为海归提供推荐服务

国家人事部留学人员和专家服务中心已开展"海外留学人员回国工作或创业推荐"业务。希望回国工作或创业的海外留学人员可及时联系该服务处。

Useful words and expressions:

人事部(人事部) [rénshìbù]: human resource department

海歸(海归) [hǎiguī]: people who have studied or worked abroad but have now returned to China.

留學人員(留学人员) [liúxué rényuán]: people who study abroad

專家(专家) [zhuānjiā]: expert

開展(开展) [kāizhǎn]: to carry out

海外(海外) [hǎiwài]: overseas

創業(创业) [chuàngyè]: to start a business

及時(及时) [jíshí]: timely

聯繫(联系) [liánxì]: to contact

該(该) [gāi]: this or that

問題(问题):

1. What service has the 人事部服務中心(人事部服务中心) started to offer?

_____

2. Where can 海外留學人員(海外留学人员) find these services?

_____

3. Translate the headlines and passage into English.

_____

_____

_____

_____

_____

V. Comprehensive exercises

For several months you have been busy searching for jobs because you are graduating in two months. Now you have a job offer, so you feel relieved. You have not written to your good friend 小華(小华) for quite a while. She is studying at another university and will graduate next year. Now you write to tell her your good news. Follow the requirements below:

1. Explain why you have not written for so long
2. Describe the job you have found
3. Ask about her plans for the summer.
4. Write at least 250 words
5. Use as many words and expressions from the lesson as you can

_____

_____

_____

_____

_____

_____

_____

_____

_____

_____

Lesson 20   I'd Rather Go on Studying Than Wait – Review
第二十課 與其等待, 不如去讀書–復習
(第二十课 与其等待, 不如去读书–复习)

I. Listening exercises

王明(王明) is graduating very soon. He has been admitted into a graduate program at 中華大學(中华大学). He is so excited that he goes to see 李老師(李老师) to thank him for his help and support. Listen to the conversation between them and then decide whether the following statements are correct or not. Put a ✔ for a correct statement and an ✗ for an incorrect one.

Useful words and expressions:

知識(知识) [zhīshi]: knowledge

祝賀(祝贺) [zhùhè]: to congratulate

懂得(懂得) [dǒngde]: to understand

安排(安排) [ānpái]: to arrange

解決(解决) [jiějué]: to solve

驕傲(骄傲) [jiāo' ào]: proud; arrogant

為……感到驕傲(为……感到骄傲) [wèi . . . gǎndào jiāo' ào]: to be proud of . . .

1. ( ) 王明沒有得到李老師的幫助, 所以研究生院沒有錄取他。
   ( ) 王明没有得到李老师的帮助, 所以研究生院没有录取他。

2. ( ) 李老師很擔心王明會他考不上研究生院。
   ( ) 李老师很担心王明会他考不上研究生院。

3. ( ) 因為李老師幫王明申請到研究生院了, 所以他非常感謝李老師。
   ( ) 因为李老师帮王明申请到研究生院了, 所以他非常感谢李老师。

4. ( ) 王明不但學習好, 而且還有很多工作經驗。
   ( ) 王明不但学习好, 而且还有很多工作经验。

5. ( ) 雖然王明非常忙, 但是他把時間安排得很好, 沒有影響學習。
   ( ) 虽然王明非常忙, 但是他把时间安排得很好, 没有影响学习。

6. ( ) 李老師教了王明怎麼做人, 可是沒有教他知識。
   ( ) 李老师教了王明怎么做人, 可是没有教他知识。

7. (　) 李老師告訴王明不要把問題留到明天。
   (　) 李老师告诉王明不要把问题留到明天。

8. (　) 李老師覺得王明的父母很驕傲。
   (　) 李老师觉得王明的父母很骄傲。

II. Character and vocabulary exercises

A. Write the traditional form of the following simplified characters:

◯　◯　◯　◯　◯　◯　◯　◯　◯

| 继 | 乐 | 紧 | 奋 | 兴 | 选 | 与 | 续 | 验 |

B. Complete the following sentences with an appropriate word chosen from the list given:

既(既)，與(兴)，經(经)，繼(继)，與(与)，即(即)，福(福)

1. 他打算畢業以後＿＿ 續去讀研究生院。

   他打算毕业以后 ＿＿ 续去读研究生院。

2. ＿＿ 其明天再做功課，不如今天晚上把它做完，明天可以去打球。

   ＿＿ 其明天再做功课，不如今天晚上把它做完，明天可以去打球。

3. 哪個公司的 ＿＿ 利待遇比較好？

   哪个公司的 ＿＿ 利待遇比较好？

4. 現在的 ＿＿ 濟情況不是太好，就業市場不太樂觀。

   现在的 ＿＿ 济情况不是太好，就业市场不太乐观。

5. 這幾天他 ＿＿ 奮極了，因為他得到了好幾個面試的機會。

   这几天他 ＿＿ 奋极了，因为他得到了好几个面试的机会。

6. ＿＿ 然我決定去那個公司了，我就更要好好地了解一下公司的

情況。

＿＿ 然我决定去那个公司了，我就更要好好地了解一下公司的

情况。

7. 我想請他們多給我一些工資，＿＿ 使他們不同意，也沒有關係。

我想请他们多给我一些工资，＿＿ 使他们不同意，也没有关系。

C. You have learned quite a few idiomatic expressions often used in spoken Chinese. Now help your friend fill in each blank below with an appropriate expression that fits the context:

1. 這個公司的年薪和福利待遇都不太好，＿＿＿＿＿＿學費補貼了。

这个公司的年薪和福利待遇都不太好，＿＿＿＿＿＿学费补贴了。

2. 我不知道該申請工作還是去讀研究生院。你給我＿＿＿＿＿＿吧。

我不知道该申请工作还是去读研究生院。你给我＿＿＿＿＿＿吧。

III. Grammar exercises

A. For each sentence below, put a ✔ if the conjunction is correct, or an ✗ if the conjunction is incorrect. If the conjunction is incorrect, please write the correct conjunction in the parentheses after the sentence:

1. ( ) 既然他們的工資低一些，我也要去那兒，因為我喜歡那兒
的工作。(____)

( ) 既然他们的工资低一些，我也要去那儿，因为我喜欢那儿
的工作。(____)

2. ( ) 即使找一個跟專業沒有關係的工作，不如再等一年。(____)

( ) 即使找一个跟专业没有关系的工作，不如再等一年。(____)

3. ( ) 與其你們都是好朋友，那就不要客氣了。(____)

( ) 与其你们都是好朋友，那就不要客气了。(____)

4. ( ) 找工作時一定要了解一下那兒的同事關係，以免以後不
高興。( )

( ) 找工作时一定要了解一下那儿的同事关系，以免以后不
高兴。( )

5. ( ) 與其去退貨，不如再買一個新的。( )
( ) 与其去退货，不如再买一个新的。( )

B. Translate the following sentences into Chinese, using the prepositions 對(对)，為(为)，
and 給(给):

1. Thank you for buying the CD for me. I am very interested in this kind of music.

_____

2. The professor wrote several letters of recommendation for me. I am really thankful to
him.

_____

3. Please introduce some good websites to me. I need some job information.

_____

IV. Media literacy reading exercises

Please read the following news article with the help of a dictionary, and then answer the
questions:

(繁體字)

首屆中國青年文化週將舉行

一場全球最大規模的華人青少年聚會－"青春中華"首屆中國
青年文化週，本月7日將在深圳拉開帷幕。屆時，來自海內外的萬餘
名青少年將會聚深圳，參與豐富多彩的文化活動。

(简体字)

首届中国青年文化周将举行

　　一场全球最大规模的华人青少年聚会－"青春中华"首届中国青年文化周，本月7日将在深圳拉开帷幕。届时，来自海内外的万余名青少年将会聚深圳，参与丰富多彩的文化活动。

Useful words and expressions:

首屆(首届) [shǒujiè]: first time
青年(青年) [qīngnián]: youth
文化(文化) [wénhuà]: culture
舉行(举行) [jǔxíng]: to hold
全球(全球) [quánqiú]: global
規模(规模) [guīmó]: size, scale
華人(华人) [huárén]: Chinese people
青少年(青少年) [qīngshàonián]: youth and teenagers
聚會(聚会) [jùhuì]: to gather
本月(本月) [běnyuè]: this month
深圳(深圳) [Shēnzhèn]: Shenzhen, a city in southern China
拉開帷幕(拉开帷幕) [lākāi wéimù]: to open the curtain
屆時(届时) [jièshí]: at that time
萬(万) [wàn]: ten thousand
餘(余) [yú]: over
參與(参与) [cānyù]: to participate
豐富多彩(丰富多彩) [fēngfùduōcǎi]: rich and versatile

問題(问题):

1. Why did thousands of young people gather at Shenzhen?

_____

2. What is a "文化週(文化周)"?

_____

3. Explain the following expressions:

a. 萬餘名(万余名) _____

b. 拉開帷幕(拉开帷幕) _____

c. 屆時(届时) _____

V. Comprehensive exercises

Listen to the conversation between 王明(王明) and 李老師(李老师) again (in the Listening exercises section). Summarize their conversation in a short essay of around 250 words. Make sure you cover all the important information.

_____

_____

_____

_____

_____

_____

_____

_____

被 ①	bèi: (particle) for passive sense sentences 被撞了 ②	yī 衣 (衤) clothing ⑥	被 被 被 ⑦		
	被 ③ 被 ④	⑧			
亠 ② 衤 ⑤	衤 衤 衤	衤 衤 衤 被			

顧 ①	gù: look, consider 照顧 ②	yè 頁 head ⑥	顧 顧 顧 ⑦		
	顧 ③ 顾 ④	⑧			
厂 户 ⑤	戶 雇 雇	雇 雇 顧			

顾 ①	gù: look, consider 照顾 ②	yè 頁 (页) head ⑥	顾 顾 顾 ⑦		
	顧 ③ 顾 ④	⑧			
厂 厅 ⑤	厄 厄 顾	顾 顾			

1) Character with its stroke order indicated by numbers

2) Pinyin pronunciation, grammatical usage, and example sentence or phrase

3) Traditional form of the character

4) Simplified form of the character

5) Stroke order illustrated by writing the character progressively

6) Radical of the character with its Pinyin pronunciation and meaning

7) Ghosted images for students to trace over

8) Dotted graph lines to aid students' practice

Note:

Detailed information is presented once for characters with no difference between traditional and simplified forms (e.g. 被). For characters which have different traditional and simplified forms (including such subtle differences as different radicals or stroke order) detailed information will first be presented for the traditional character, and then for its simplified counterpart (e.g. 顧 and 顾).

Lesson 15   I Have No Choice but to Ask for Your Help – Review

第十五課 我只好求你幫忙–復習
(第十五课 我只好求你帮忙–复习)

求	qiú: beg 求你幫忙	shuǐ 水 (氵) water	求 求 求
	求 求		
一 丁 扌 求 求			

求	qiú: beg 求你帮忙	yī 一 one	求 求 求
	求 求		
一 丁 扌 求 求			

磁	cí: magnet 磁带(带)	shí 石 stone	磁 磁 磁
	磁 磁		
厂 石 石丷 矽丷 磁 磁			

聯	lián: connect 聯係	ěr 耳 ear	聯	聯	聯
聯 联					
耳	耵	聯	聯	聯	聯	聯	聯

联	lián: connect 联系	ěr 耳 ear	联	联	联
聯 联					
ㄇ	耳	耵	联	联			

絡	luò: to wrap around; a net 聯絡	mì 系 (糹) silk	絡	絡	絡
絡 络					
糸	絞	絡			

络	luò: to wrap around; a net 联络	mì 系 (纟) silk	络	络	络
絡 络					
纟	纱	纹	络		

卻	**què: but** 想做卻沒做	**jié ㄗ** joint	卻 卻 卻	
	卻 却			
八 父 谷 谷卩 卻				

却	**què: but** 想做却没做	**jié ㄗ** joint	却 却 却	
	卻 却			
土 去 去卩 却				

遇	**yù: meet** 遇到麻煩(烦)事	**chuò 辵(辶)** motion	遇 遇 遇	
	遇 遇			
日 昌 禺 禺 禺 遇 遇				

錄	**lù: record** 錄音機	**jīn 金** metal	錄 錄 錄	
	錄 录			
人 今 金 釒 釚 釞 鋖 錄				

录

		lù: record 录音机		jì ㄐ snout		录	录	录
		錄	录					
フ	ㄐ	彐	寻	录				

絞

		jiǎo: wring 絞磁帶		mì 系(糸) silk		絞	絞	絞
		絞	絞					
纟	糸	紅	紁	紡	絞			

绞

		jiǎo: wring 绞磁带		mì 系(纟) silk		绞	绞	绞
		绞	绞					
纟	纟	纟	纺	绞				

力

		lì: strength (用力: put forth one's strength)		lì 力 strength		力	力	力
		力	力					
フ	力							

反	fǎn: in reverse (反而: on the contrary)		yòu 又 right hand		反	反	反
	反	反					
厂	厂	反					

遍	biàn: all over 找遍了		chuò 辵 (辶) motion		遍	遍	遍
	遍	遍					
丶	二	户	户	扁	遍	遍	

碟	dié: disc 光碟		shí 石 stone		碟	碟	碟
	碟	碟					
石	石	矿	碟	碟	碟		

歌	gē: song 流行歌		qiàn 欠 owe		歌	歌	歌
	歌	歌					
戸	可	可	哥	哥	歌	歌	歌

流	liú: flow, current 流行	shuǐ 水 (氵) water	流	流	流
	流	流			
氵	汀	沄	浐	流	

搜	sōu: search 搜索	shǒu 手 (扌) hand	搜	搜	搜
	搜	搜			
扌	扌	扌	护	护	押	押	搜

索	suǒ: search 搜(搜)索	mì 糸 (纟) silk	索	索	索
	索	索			
十	屯	宏	索		

購	gòu: purchase 求購	bèi 貝 shell	購	購	購
	購	购			
目	貝	貝艹	貝艹	購	購	購	購

购	gòu: purchase 求购	bèi 貝 (贝) shell	购	购	购
	購 购				
冂	刀	贝	贝 购		

帖	tiě: card note 帖子	jīn 巾 napkin	帖	帖	帖
	帖 帖				
冂	巾	忄 帖			

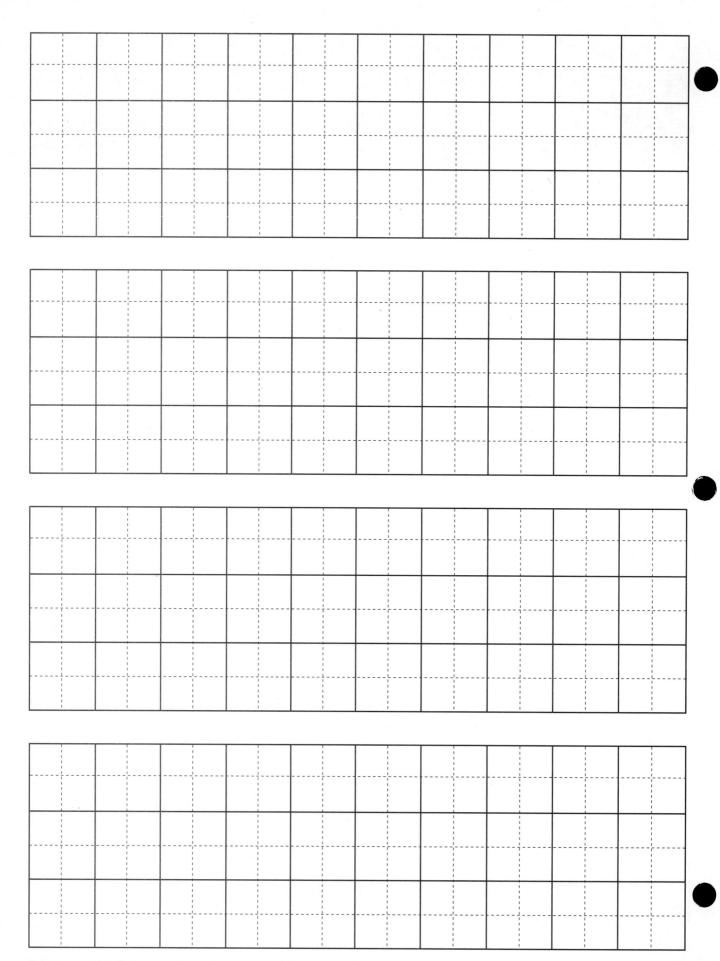

第十五課 ■ 我只好……復習 (第十五课 ■ 我只好……复习)　Lesson 15 ■ *I Have No Choice . . . Review*

Lesson 16　We Must Come to Visit You
第十六課　我們非過來看您不可
(第十六课　我们非过来看您不可)

級	jí: level 年級	mì 系 (糹) silk	級 級 級
	級 级		
幺　糸	糿　紒　級		

级	jí: level 年级	mì 系 (纟) silk	级 级 级
	級 级		
纟　纟	纫　级		

趁	chèn: avail oneself of 趁機(机)會(会)	zǒu 走 walk	趁 趁 趁
	趁 趁		
土　丰	走　赱　赵　趁		

		dīng: (onomatopoeia) 叮噹(当)	kǒu 口 mouth	叮	叮	叮
叮		叮	叮			
口	口一	叮				

		dāng: (onomatopoeia) 叮噹	kǒu 口 mouth	噹	噹	噹
噹		噹	当			
口	口ᵘ	哳	啙	噹		

		dāng: (onomatopoeia) 叮当	xiǎo 小 small	当	当	当
当		噹	当			
ᵘ	业	当	当			

		líng: bell 門鈴	jīn 金 metal	鈴	鈴	鈴
鈴		鈴	铃			
金	釒	鈴	鈴			

铃		líng: bell 门铃	jīn 金 (钅) metal	铃	铃	铃
		鈴 铃				
ノ	钅	钅 铃 铃 铃				

響		xiǎng: sound, ring 門鈴響了	yīn 音 sound	響	響	響
		響 响				
乡	狚	绑 響 響 響				

响		xiǎng: sound, ring 门铃响了	kǒu 口 mouth	响	响	响
		響 响				
口	叮	叻 响				

提		tí: carry, refer to 提起	shǒu 手 (扌) hand	提	提	提
		提 提				
扌	护	挕 挕 提				

括	kuò: include 包括	shǒu 手 (扌) hand	括 括 括
	括 括		
扌 扩 扩 括			

世	shì: world, life 待人處(处)世	yī 一 one	世 世 世
	世 世		
十 卅 卅 世			

寶	bǎo: treasure 寶貴	mián 宀 roof	寶 寶 寶
	寶 宝		
宀 宁 宨 宲 窀 窑 寍 寶			

宝	bǎo: treasure 宝贵	mián 宀 roof	宝 宝 宝
	寶 宝		
宀 宁 宇 宝 宝			

懂	dǒng: understand 懂得道理	xīn 心 (忄) heart	懂 懂 懂
懂 懂			
忄 忙 怦 惜 惜 懂 懂			

懂	dǒng: understand 懂得道理	xīn 心 (忄) heart	懂 懂 懂
懂 懂			
忄 忙 怦 惜 惜 懂 懂			

佩	pèi: admire 佩服	rén 人 (亻) person	佩 佩 佩
佩 佩			
亻 仉 伵 佩 佩			

齊	qí: uniform 看齊	qí 齊 uniform	齊 齊 齊
齊 齐			
亠 六 亠 亣 亣 亝 旅 旅 齊 齊			

齐	qí: uniform 看齐	qí 齐 uniform	齐 齐 齐
	齊 齐		
一 文 文 齐			

繼	jì: continue 繼續	mì 糸 (糹) silk	繼 繼 繼
	繼 继		
糸 糹 糸丝 糸丝 糸丝 糸丝 繼			

继	jì: continue 继续	mì 糸 (纟) silk	继 继 继
	繼 继		
纟 纟 纟半 纟米 继			

續	xù: continue 繼續	mì 糸 (糹) silk	續 續 續
	續 续		
糸 糸 績 繢 續			

续

		xù: continue 继续		**mì** 系 (纟) silk		续	续	续

績 续

纟 | 纟⁺ | 纱 | 绉 | 续

讀

dú: read, study 讀硕士		**yán** 言 word		讀	讀	讀

讀 读

言 | 訁 | 讠 | 讀 | 讀

读

dú: read, study 读硕士		**yán** 言 (讠) word		读	读	读

讀 读

讠 | 讠⁺ | 讠 | 读 | 读

濟

jì: aid, help 經濟學		**shuǐ** 水 (氵) water		濟	濟	濟

濟 济

氵 | 氵 | 濟 | 濟

济

jì: aid, help
经济学

shuǐ 水 (氵)
water

济 济 济

濟 济

氵 冫 沪 汯 济

硕

shuò: large
硕士

shí 石
stone

硕 硕 硕

硕 硕

石 石 矴 硔 硕

硕

shuò: large
硕士

shí 石
stone

硕 硕 硕

硕 硕

石 石 矴 硕 硕

授

shòu: teach
教授

shǒu 手 (扌)
hand

授 授 授

授 授

扌 扩 扩 护 授

將	jiāng: support (將來: future)	cùn 寸 inch	將	將	將
	將 將				
㇄	丩 丬 㣺 㣺 將				

将	jiāng: support (将来: future)	cùn 寸 inch	将	将	将
	將 将				
丶	丬 丬 㣺 㣺 将				

途	tú: road, route 前途無(无)量	chuò 辵(辶) motion	途	途	途
	途 途				
人	今 仐 余 诠 途				

無	wú: without 前途無量	huǒ 火 (灬) fire	無	無	無
	無 无				
㇒	亾 𠂉 缶 無 無				

无	wú: without 前途无量	wú 无 without	无	无	无
無 无					
一 二 干 无					

量	liàng: measure 前途無(无)量	lǐ 里 inner	量	量	量
量 量					
日 旦 昌 昌 量 量					

獎	jiǎng: award 過獎	quǎn 犬(犭) dog	獎	獎	獎
獎 奖					
爿 爿' 爿' 將 將 獎 獎					

奖	jiǎng: award 过奖	dà 大 big	奖	奖	奖
獎 奖					
丬 丬 爿 爿 奖					

講

jiǎng: speak
講講計畫

yán 言
word

講 講 講

講 讲

言　言　訁　講　講　講

讲

jiǎng: speak
讲讲计划

yán 言 (讠)
word

讲 讲 讲

講 讲

讠　讠　讠　讲　讲

驗

yàn: examine
經驗

mǎ 馬
horse

驗 驗 驗

驗 验

丨　厂　厈　厈　馬　馬　馬　驗　驗　驗

验

yàn: examine
经验

mǎ 馬 (马)
horse

验 验 验

驗 验

フ　马　马　驴　驴　验　验

磨 (1-16)	**mó: grind** 磨练	**shí 石** stone	磨	磨	磨
	磨 磨				
广	床	麻	麻	庳	磨

番 (1-12)	**fān: (M.W. for cause)** 做一番事業(业)	**tián 田** land	番	番	番
	番 番				
一	平	乎	采	番	

油 (1-8)	**yóu: oil, gasoline** 加油	**shuǐ 水 (氵)** water	油	油	油
	油 油				
氵	沪	泂	油	油	

擾 (1-18)	**rǎo: harass, trouble** 打擾	**shǒu 手 (扌)** hand	擾	擾	擾
	擾 扰				
扌	扩	护	捛	掁	撋 撄 擾

		rǎo: harass, trouble 打扰	shǒu 手(扌) hand	扰 扰 扰		

擾 扰

扌 扩 扩 扰 扰

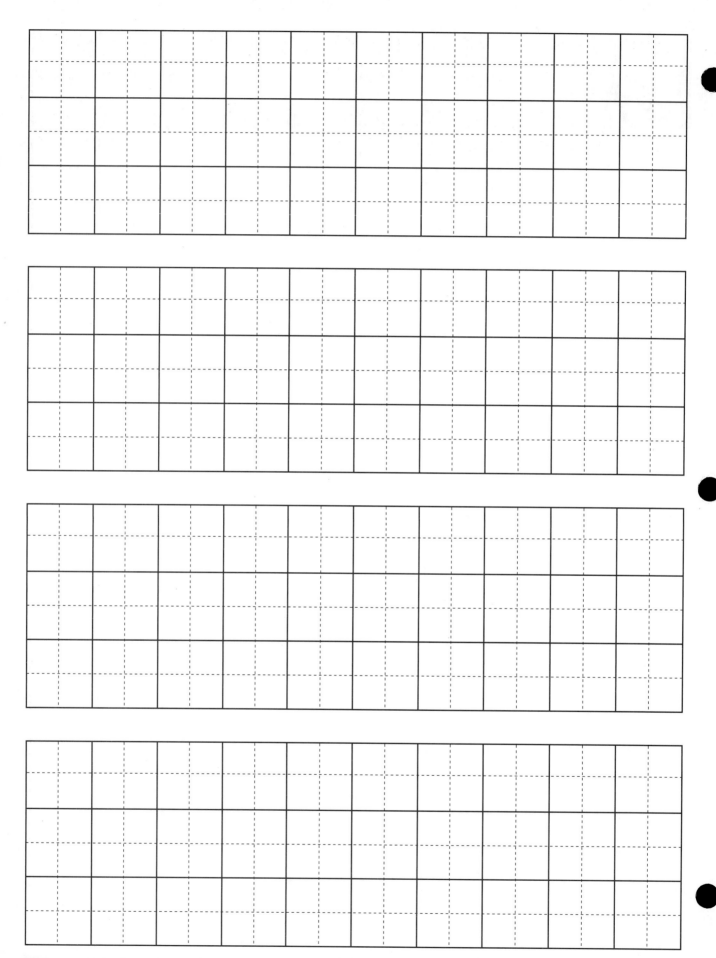

第十六課 ■ 我們非過來看您不可 (第十六课 ■ 我们非过来看您不可)　**Lesson 16** ■ *We Must Come to Visit You*

Lesson 17   Didn't You Apply for an Internship Last Year?
第十七課　你難道不是去年申請實習了嗎？
(第十七课　你难道不是去年申请实习了吗？)

簡	jiǎn: brief 簡歷	zhú 竹 (⺮) bamboo	簡	簡	簡
	簡	简			
⺮	⺮	𥫗	𥫗	𥫗	節	節	簡

简	jiǎn: brief 简历	zhú 竹 (⺮) bamboo	简	简	简
	簡	简			
⺮	⺮	𥫗	𥫗	简

複	fù: complex, complicated 複雜	yī 衣 (衤) clothing	複	複	複
	複	复			
衤	衤	袖	袧	複

復		fù: complex, complicated 复杂	pū 攴 (攵) literacy	复	复	复
	複 复					
㇀	白	旬	复			

雜		zá: miscellaneous, mixed 複雜	zhuī 隹 bird tail	雜	雜	雜
	雜 杂					
亠	六	众	杂	刹	雜	雜

杂		zá: miscellaneous, mixed 复杂	mù 木 wood	杂	杂	杂
	雜 杂					
ノ	九	杂				

首		shǒu: head, first 首先	shǒu 首 head	首	首	首
	首 首					
㇀	艹	艹	首	首		

質	zhì: quality, nature 質量	bèi 貝 shell	質 質 質
	質 质		
厂 斤 乕 斦 皙 質			

质	zhì: quality, nature 质量	bèi 貝 (贝) shell	质 质 质
	質 质		
厂 斤 斦 质 质			

調	tiáo: adjust 調整	yán 言 word	調 调 调
	調 调		
言 訁 訂 調 調			

调	tiáo: adjust 调整	yán 言 (讠) word	调 调 调
	調 调		
讠 订 讥 调 调			

		tū: stick out 突出	xué 穴 cave	突	突	突
突		突	突			
宀	穴	突	突			

		jù: reject 拒絕(绝)	shǒu 手(扌) hand	拒	拒	拒
拒		拒	拒			
扌	扩	扩	护	拒	拒	

		jué: absolutely, make no allowance 拒絕	mì 糸(糹) silk	絕	絕	絕
絕		絕	绝			
糸	紉	絽	紹	紹	絕	

		jué: absolutely, make no allowance 拒绝	mì 糸(纟) silk	绝	绝	绝
绝		絕	绝			
纟	纠	纺	绉	绝		

仔	zǐ: small and fine 仔細(细)	rén 人 (亻) person	仔	仔	仔
	仔	仔			
亻	亻	仔	仔		

細	xì: thin, fine 仔細	mì 系 (糸) silk	細	細	細
	細	細			
糸	紀	紐	細	細	

细	xì: thin, fine 仔細	mì 系 (纟) silk	细	细	细
	細	细			
纟	纠	细			

修	xiū: repair, trim 修改	rén 人 (亻) person	修	修	修
	修	修			
亻	亻	亻	修	修	

修	xiū: repair, trim 修改	rén 人 (亻) person	修	修	修
	修	修			
亻	亻	修	修		

招	zhāo: attract, recruit 招工	shǒu 手 (扌) hand	招	招	招
	招	招			
扌	扌	扫	招		

聘	pìn: engage, hire 招聘	ěr 耳 ear	聘	聘	聘
	聘	聘			
一	丌	耳	耶	聒	聘

格	gé: case 表格	mù 木 wood	格	格	格
	格	格			
木	术	杉	权	格	

162 第十七課 ■ 你難道不是……? (第十七课 ■ 你难道不是……?)　　Lesson 17 ■ *Didn't You Apply for . . . ?*

Name: _____ Date: _____

薦	jiàn: recommend 推薦	cǎo 艸 (艹) grass	薦	薦	薦
	薦 荐				
艹	产 芦 萨 荐 薦 薦				

荐	jiàn: recommend 推荐	cǎo 艸 (艹) grass	荐	荐	荐
	薦 荐				
艹	艼 芦 芢 荐 荐				

恐	kǒng: fear 恐怕	xīn 心 (忄) heart	恐	恐	恐
	恐 恐				
工	卫 巩 巩 恐				

限	xiàn: limit, restrict 有限	fù 阜 (阝) hill	限	限	限
	限 限				
阝	阝 阝 阻 限 限				

第十七課 ▪ 你難道不是……?（第十七课 ▪ 你难道不是……?）　Lesson 17 ▪ *Didn't You Apply for . . . ?*　163

慮 (lǜ: consider)

慮	lǜ: consider 考慮	xīn 心(忄) heart	慮	慮	慮
	慮	虍			
卜	上	广	卢	虍	慮

虑 (lǜ: consider)

虑	lǜ: consider 考慮	xīn 心(忄) heart	虑	虑	虑
	慮	虑			
卜	上	户	卢	虎	虑

聰 (cōng: acute hearing)

聰	cōng: acute hearing 聰明	ěr 耳 ear	聰	聰	聰
	聰	聪			
丌	耳	耵	耵	聊	聰

聪 (cōng: acute hearing)

聪	cōng: acute hearing 聪明	ěr 耳 ear	聪	聪	聪
	聰	聪			
丌	耳	耵	耴	聪	

		gàn: do, work 能幹	gān　干 shield	幹 幹 幹
幹	幹 干			
十	古 卓	乾 幹		

		gàn: do, work 能干	gān　干 shield	干 干 干
干	幹 干			
一	二 干			

		yuàn: desire, wish 但願	yè　頁 head	願 願 願
願	願 愿			
厂	厃 厵 原 願			

		yuàn: desire, wish 但愿	xīn　心（忄） heart	愿 愿 愿
愿	願 愿			
厂	厂 厃 原 愿			

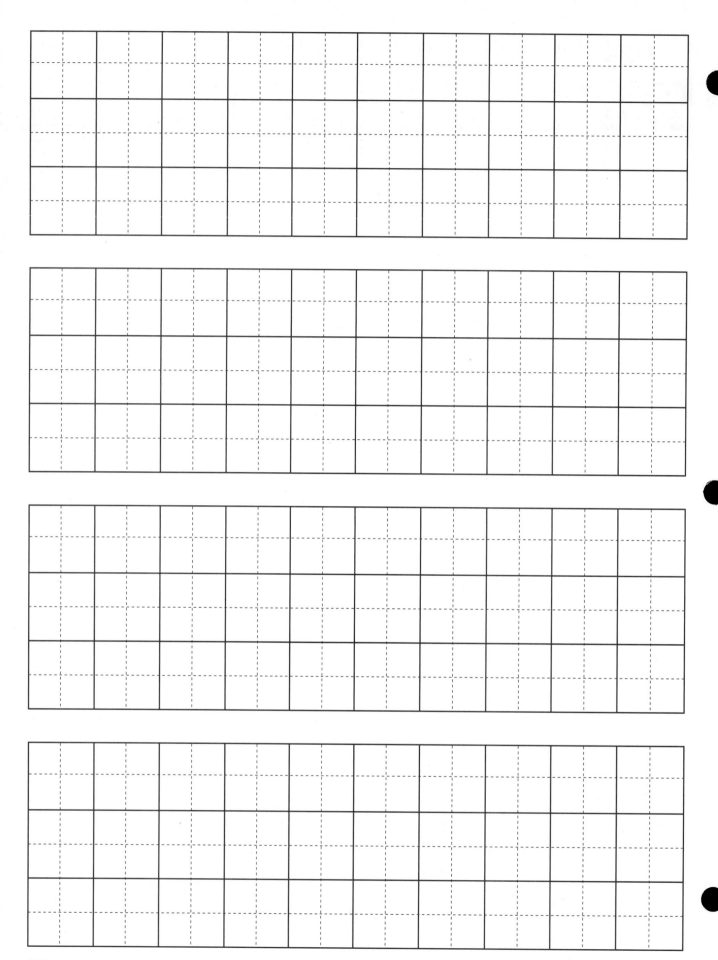

Name: _____ Date: _____

Lesson 18   The Company Has Around 300 Employees
第十八課 公司的員工有三百個左右
(第十八课 公司的员工有三百个左右)

任	rèn: appoint, official post 主任	rén 人(亻) person	任	任	任
	任 任				
亻 任 任					

科	kē: section, science 科學(学)	hé 禾 grain	科	科	科
	科 科				
禾 禾 科 科					

份	fèn: (M.W. for jobs) 一份工作	rén 人(亻) person	份	份	份
	份 份				
亻 价 份 份					

		zī: consult 咨詢(询)	kǒu 口 mouth	咨	咨	咨
咨	咨 咨					
`	`` 次 咨					

		xún: inquire 詢問	yán 言 word	詢	詢	詢
詢	詢 询					
言 言	訁 詢					

		xún: inquire 询问	yán 言(讠) word	询	询	询
询	詢 询					
讠 讠	讠 询					

		ruǎn: soft 软件	chē 車 vehicle	軟	軟	軟
軟	軟 软					
車 軒	軒 軟					

软	ruǎn: soft 软件	chē 车(车) vehicle	软	软	软
	软	软				
一	土	车	车	轩	软	

供	gōng: supply 提供	rén 人(亻) person	供	供	供
	供	供				
亻	什	仕	供	供		

儘	jǐn: despite 儘管	rén 人(亻) person	儘	儘	儘
	儘	尽				
亻	伊	伊	儘	儘	儘	儘

尽	jǐn: despite 尽管	shī 尸 corpse	尽	尽	尽
	儘	尽				
ㄱ	ㄱ	尸	尺	尽		

除	**chú: except** 除了學(学)習(习)以外， 我還(还)喜歡(欢)旅行	**fù 阜 (阝)** hill
	除 除	
阝 阝\ 阶 除 除		

副	**fù: assistant** 副修	**dāo 刀 (刂)** knife
	副 副	
口 畐 副 副		

均	**jūn: equal** 平均	**tǔ 土** earth
	均 均	
土 圤 均 均 均		

績	**jì: achievement** 成績	**mì 糸 (糹)** silk
	績 绩	
糸 糸ᵀ 絆 結 績		

		jì: achievement 成绩	mì 系(纟) silk	绩	绩	绩

绩 | 绩 | | | | |

纟 | 纟 | 纟 | 纟 | 绩 | |

| | | céng: ever 曾經(经) | yuē 曰 say | 曾 | 曾 | 曾 |

曾 | 曾 | | | | |

丷 | 丷 | 兯 | 冎 | 甶 | 曾 |

| | | jiā: praise 嘉獎(奖) | kǒu 口 mouth | 嘉 | 嘉 | 嘉 |

嘉 | 嘉 | | | | |

士 | 吉 | 壴 | 壴 | 亯 | 嘉 | 嘉 |

| | | zǔ: group 組織 | mì 系(纟) silk | 組 | 組 | 組 |

組 | 组 | | | | |

糸 | 糹 | 糽 | 組 | 組 |

组	zǔ: group 组织		mì 系 (纟) silk		组	组	组
	組	组					
纟	纠	纫	组	组			

織	zhī: knit 組織		mì 系 (纟) silk		織	織	織
	織	织					
糸	糸	紅	経	縮	織	織	織

织	zhī: knit 组织		mì 系 (纟) silk		织	织	织
	織	织					
纟	纫	织					

凡	fán: every, ordinary 凡是		zhǔ ` segmentation symbol		凡	凡	凡
	凡	凡					
丿	几	凡					

172 第十八課 ▪ 公司的員工有…… (第十八课 ▪ 公司的员工有……)   Lesson 18 ▪ *The Company Has . . .*

凡	fán: every, ordinary 凡是	jī 几 bench	凡 凡 凡
凡	凡 凡		
ノ 几 凡			

項	xiàng: item, term 項目	yè 頁 head	項 項 項
項	項 項		
工 工 项 項			

项	xiàng: item, term 項目	yè 頁 (页) head	项 项 项
项	项 项		
工 工 项 项 项			

目	mù: eye 目標(标)	mù 目 eye	目 目 目
目	目 目		
冂 冂 目 目			

		lùn: discuss, statement 論文			yán 言 word		論	論	論
論		論	论							
言	訐	訡	論	論						

		lùn: discuss, statement 论文			yán 言(讠) word		论	论	论
论		論	论							
讠	论	讼	论							

Lesson 19　I Would Rather Go to the Financial Bank
第十九課　我倒寧願去金融銀行
(第十九课　我倒宁愿去金融银行)

寧	nìng: rather 寧願		mián 宀 roof	寧	寧	寧
	寧	宁				
宀 忘	寍	寍	寍	寧		

宁	nìng: rather 宁愿		mián 宀 roof	宁	宁	宁
	寧	宁				
宀 宁 宁						

融	róng: melt 融洽		chóng 虫 worm	融	融	融
	融	融				
口 鬲 鬲 鬲 鬲 鬲口 融 融						

競

		jìng: contest 競爭		lì 立 stand		競	競	競
		競	竞					
立	音	竞	竟	䇞	競			

竞

		jìng: contest 竞争		lì 立 stand		竞	竞	竞
		競	竞					
立	音	竜	竞					

爭

		zhēng: contend 競爭		zhǎo 爪 (⺥) claw		爭	爭	爭
		爭	争					
⼂	⺈	爫	乊	乊	爭			

争

		zhēng: contend 竞争		dāo 刀 (刂) knife		争	争	争
		爭	争					
⺈	⺈	乌	争	争				

賀	hè: congratulate 祝賀	bèi 貝 shell	賀	賀	賀
	賀	賀			
ㄱ	力	加	智	賀	

贺	hè: congratulate 祝贺	yè 頁(页) head	贺	贺	贺
	贺	贺			
力	加	贺	贺		

謙	qiān: modest 謙虛	yán 言 word	謙	謙	謙
	謙	谦			
言	言	詳	謙	謙	謙	謙

谦	qiān: modest 谦虚	yán 言(讠) word	谦	谦	谦
	谦	谦			
讠	讠	讠	谦	谦	谦

虚	xū: void, humble 謙虛	hū 虍 tiger's stripes	虚	虚	虚
虚	虚				
卜 广 庐	虎 虚	虚	虚	虚	

虛	xū: void, humble 谦虚	hū 虍 tiger's stripes	虛	虛	虛
虛	虛				
卜 广 庐	虎 虚	虚	虚	虛	

資	zī: expenses, money 工資	bèi 貝 shell	資	資	資
資	資				
冫 氵 次	資 資				

资	zī: expenses, money 工资	bèi 貝 (贝) shell	资	资	资
资	资				
冫 氵 次	咨 资				

穩	wěn: steady 穩定	hé 禾 grain	穩 穩 穩
禾 秆 秆 穏 穩	穩 穩		

稳	wěn: steady 稳定	hé 禾 grain	稳 稳 稳
禾 秆 稳 稳	穩 稳		

薪	xīn: salary, firewood 年薪	cǎo 艸 (艹) grass	薪 薪 薪
艹 芓 莘 薪 薪 薪 薪	薪 薪		

薪	xīn: salary, firewood 年薪	cǎo 艸 (艹) grass	薪 薪 薪
艹 芓 莘 薪 薪 薪 薪	薪 薪		

萬

wàn: ten thousand 五萬	căo 艸 (⺾) grass	萬	萬	萬

萬 万

艹 苜 萬 萬 萬 萬

万

wàn: ten thousand 五万	yī 一 one	万	万	万

萬 万

一 丆 万

股

gǔ: section 股份	ròu 肉 (月) meat	股	股	股

股 股

月 𦩁 股

婆

pó: mother-in-law, old woman 婆婆	nǚ 女 female	婆	婆	婆

婆 婆

氵 汀 汇 沪 涉 波 婆

	jìng: complete; investigate 究竟	yīn 音 sound	竟	竟	竟
竟	竟 竟				
立	音	音	竟		

	liáo: cure, treat 醫療	nè 疒 sick	療	療	療
療	療 疗				
广	疒	疾	疾	瘩	瘩	療

	liáo: cure, treat 医疗	nè 疒 sick	股	股	股
疗	療 疗				
广	疒	疗			

	tiē: allowance 補貼	bèi 貝 shell	贴	贴	贴
贴	贴 贴				
目	貝	貼	贴		

	tiē: allowance 补贴	bèi 贝 (贝) shell	贴	贴	贴
贴	贴 贴				
冂 贝 贝丿 贴 贴					

	fú: blessing, good fortune 福利	shì 示 (礻) reveal	福	福	福
福	福 福				
礻 祀 祚 福					

	yóu: still 猶豫	quǎn 犬 (犭) dog	猶	猶	猶
猶	猶 犹				
犭 犭 犷 猫 猶 猶					

	yóu: still 犹豫	quǎn 犬 (犭) dog	犹	犹	犹
犹	猶 犹				
犭 犭 犭一 犴 犹 犹					

豫	yù: comfort, please 猶豫	shǐ 豕 pig	豫	豫	豫
豫	豫				
マ	予	予`	矛	矛	矛	豫	

豫	yù: comfort, please 犹豫	shǐ 豕 pig	豫	豫	豫
豫	豫				
予	予`	矛	孖	矛	豫	豫	豫

固	gù: solid (固然: certainly)	wéi 囗 enclosure	固	固	固
固	固				
冂	冂	同	固			

環	huán: annulus, loop 環境	yù 玉 (王) jade	環	環	環
環	环				
王	珏	珏	珏	珇	環	環	環

环	huán: annulus, loop 环境	yù 玉 (王) jade	环 环 环
二 干 王 环	環 环		

境	jìng: area, condition 環(环)境	tǔ 土 earth	境 境 境
土 圤 培 境 境	境 境		

確	què: true, firmly 確實	shí 石 stone	確 確 確
石 矿 矿 碎 確 確	確 确		

确	què: true, firmly 确实	shí 石 stone	确 确 确
石 矿 确 确 确	確 确		

洽		qià: fit, suit 融洽	shuǐ 水 (氵) water	洽	洽	洽
氵	汋	洽	洽			
		沪	泠	洽		

賺		zhuàn: gain, make a profit 賺錢	bèi 貝 shell	賺	賺	賺
		賺	賺			
目	貝	貝⺈	賆	賺	賺	賺

赚		zhuàn: gain, make a profit 赚钱	bèi 貝 (贝) shell	赚	赚	赚
		赚	赚			
贝	贝⺈	赔	赚	赚		

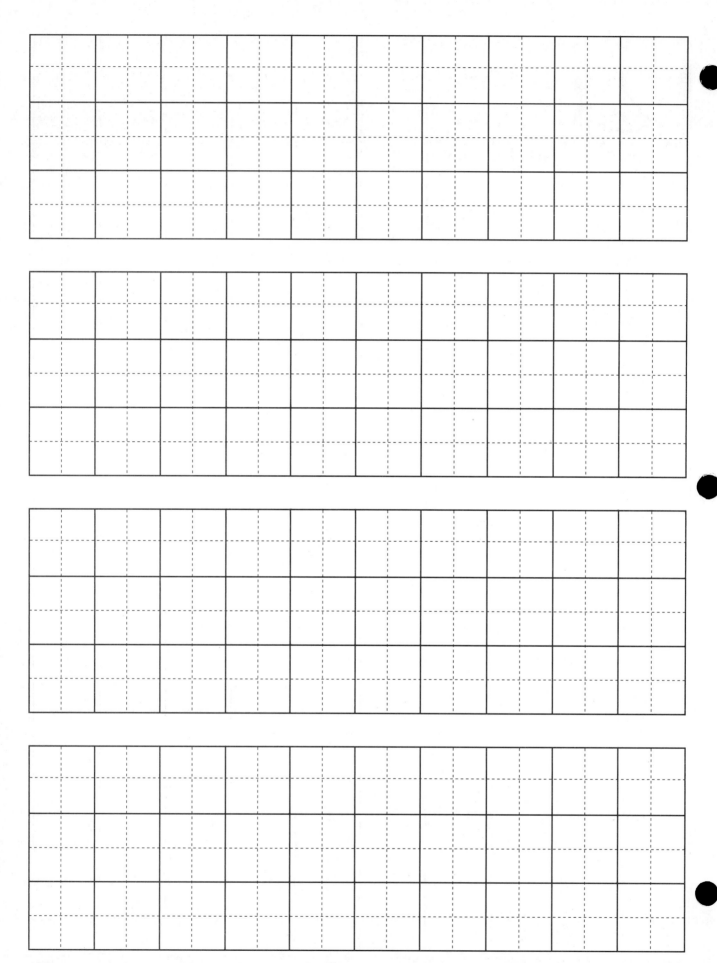

Name: ____________________ Date: ______________

Lesson 20 I'd Rather Go on Studying Than Wait – Review
第二十課 與其等待, 不如去讀書–復習
(第二十课 与其等待, 不如去读书–复习)

與	yǔ: and (與其: rather than)	jiù 臼 mortar	與	與	與
	與 与				

Stroke order: 与 与 与 与 與 與 與

与	yǔ: and (与其: rather than)	yī 一 one	与	与	与
	與 与				

Stroke order: 一 与 与

即	jí: namely 即使	jié 卩 joint	即	即	即
	即 即				

Stroke order: ㇆ ヨ 艮 即 即

	fèn: act vigorously, raise 奮鬥	dà 大 big	奮	奮	奮
奮	奮 奮				
六 奔 奞 奞 奞 奮					

	fèn: act vigorously, raise 奋斗	dà 大 big	奋	奋	奋
奋	奮 奋				
大 奋					

	tiāo: pick, select 挑選(选)	shǒu 手(扌) hand	挑	挑	挑
挑	挑 挑				
扌 扛 扒 扒 挑					

	xuǎn: elect, select 挑選	chuò 辵(辶) motion	選	選	選
選	選 选				
コ 巳 巴 毗 巽 巽 𢃻 選					

选		xuǎn: elect, select 挑选		chuò 辵 (辶) motion		选	选	选
		選	选					
丿	乍	先	选					

謀		móu: consult, plan 參謀		yán 言 word		謀	謀	謀
		謀	谋					
言	言	計	訓	謀				

谋		móu: consult, plan 参谋		yán 言 (讠) word		谋	谋	谋
		謀	谋					
讠	讠	计	训	谋				

免		miǎn: avoid 以免		ér 儿 walking man		免	免	免
		免	免					
夕	乌	免	免					

兔	miǎn: avoid 以免		dāo 刀 (⺈) knife	兔	兔	兔
	兔	兔				
⺈	刍	夕	兔			

獲	huò: win, obtain 收獲		quǎn 犬 (犭) dog	獲	獲	獲
	獲	获				
犭	犭	犭	獲	獲		

获	huò: win, obtain 收获		cǎo 艸 (艹) grass	获	获	获
	獲	获				
艹	艹	艹	荻	获	获	

鬥	dòu: fight, contest with 奮鬥		dòu 鬥 fight	鬥	鬥	鬥
	鬥	斗				
丨	丨	丆	匡	匡	匡	鬥

斗		dòu: fight, contest with 奋斗	dòu 斗 fight	斗	斗	斗
	鬥 斗					
、	二	三	斗			

標		biāo: mark 目標	mù 木 wood	標	標	標
	標 标					
木	朽	枦	柵	標		

标		biāo: mark 目标	mù 木 wood	标	标	标
	標 标					
木	朽	杅	标			

攻		gōng: study, attack 攻讀(读)	pū 攴(攵) literacy	攻	攻	攻
	攻 攻					
エ	エ	玑	玏	攻		

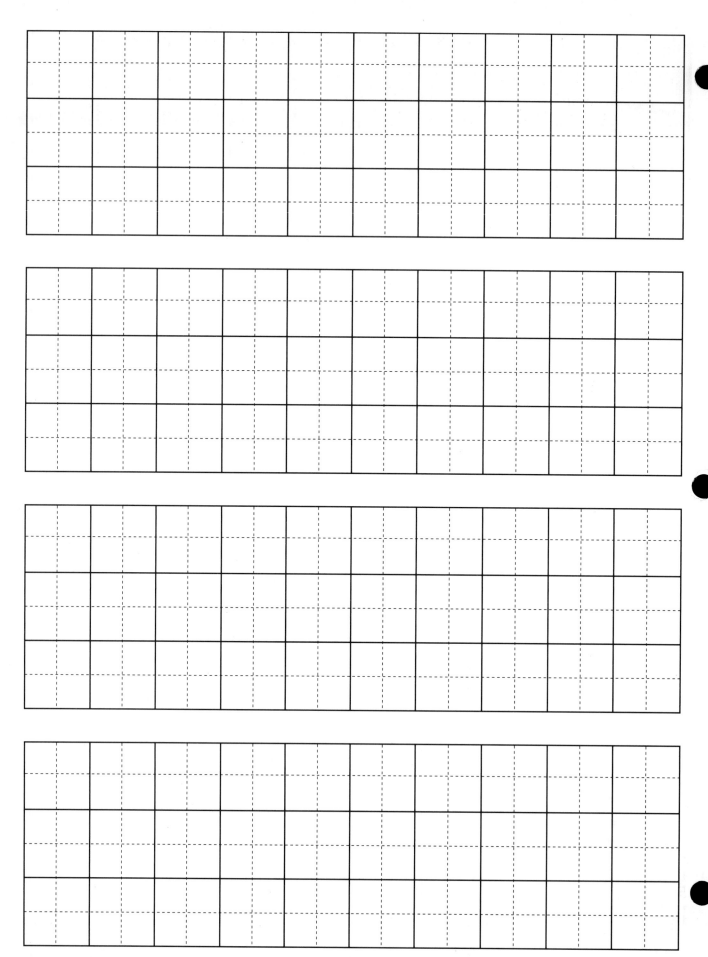

第二十課 ▪ 與其等待, ……－復習 (第二十课 ▪ 与其等待, ……－复习)　**Lesson 20** ▪ *I'd Rather Go . . . Review*

Each entry lists traditional character, simplified character, Pinyin, English meaning, and lesson number:

2

刀	刀	dāo	knife	2
又	又	yòu	again	13
力	力	lì	strength	15

3

己	己	jǐ	oneself	2
叉	叉	chā	cross	3
口	口	kǒu	mouth, entrance	3
山	山	shān	mountain	3
之	之	zhī	(a particle)	6
千	千	qiān	thousand	6
士	士	shì	person	11
凡	凡	fán	every; ordinary	18

4

片	片	piàn	thin piece	2
化	化	huà	變化: change	3
尺	尺	chǐ	ruler	3
戶	户	hù	door; (bank) account	6
支	支	zhī	to pay out; withdraw	6
元	元	yuán	dollar	6
及	及	jí	to reach, attain	7
夫	夫	fū	功夫: Kung Fu	8
引	引	yǐn	to lead, attract	8
父	父	fù	father	11
止	止	zhǐ	to stop	13
毛	毛	máo	hair	14
反	反	fǎn	in reverse	15

5

主	主	zhǔ	主意: idea	1
北	北	běi	north	2

台	台	tái	stage, platform	2
左	左	zuǒ	left	3
田	田	tián	field	3
右	右	yòu	right	3
民	民	mín	people	3
母	母	mǔ	mother	4
永	永	yǒng	forever	4
乎	乎	hū	(a particle expressing doubt or conjecture)	4
卡	卡	kǎ	card	6
它	它	tā	it	8
古	古	gǔ	ancient	8
代	代	dài	historical period; generation	8
史	史	shǐ	history	8
且	且	qiě	而且: also, in addition	8
末	末	mò	end	8
由	由	yóu	from	12
匆	匆	cōng	hurriedly	13
示	示	shì	to notify, show	14
失	失	shī	to lose	14
叮	叮	dīng	(onomatopoeia)	16
世	世	shì	world; life	16
仔	仔	zǐ	small and fine	17
目	目	mù	eye	18

6

合	合	hé	to combine	1
衣	衣	yī	clothes	1
死	死	sǐ	dead	1
各	各	gè	each, every	2
全	全	quán	whole; intact	3

交	交	jiāo	(of places or periods of time) meet, join	3
成	成	chéng	to become	3
向	向	xiàng	to, towards	3
亦	亦	yì	also	4
存	存	cún	to deposit	6
而	而	ér	而且: also, in addition	8
早	早	zǎo	early	9
吋	吋	cùn	inch	9
旬	旬	xún	a period of ten days	10
曲	曲	qū	bend, crooked	10
此	此	cǐ	this	12
至	至	zhì	to reach	12
守	守	shǒu	to guard	13
危	危	wēi	danger	14
任	任	rèn	to appoint	18
份	份	fèn	(measure word for jobs)	18

7

別	別	bié	don't	1
呀	呀	ya	(indicating surprise)	1
李	李	lǐ	行李: luggage	1
附	附	fù	be near	1
忘	忘	wàng	to forget	1
里	里	lǐ	公里: kilometer	3
利	利	lì	profit, interest	6
低	低	dī	low	6
兌	兑	duì	to exchange	6
社	社	shè	agency, society	7
告	告	gào	to notify, announce	8
完	完	wán	finish, complete	8
技	技	jì	skill	8
呎	呎	chǐ	(a unit of length) foot	9
更	更	gèng	even, more	9
希	希	xī	to hope	10
助	助	zhù	to aid, help	10
壯	壮	zhuàng	strong; grand	10
折	折	zhé	to bend, twist	10
肚	肚	dù	belly	11
束	束	shù	to bind	11
何	何	hé	why not	12

初	初	chū	at the beginning of	12
吵	吵	chǎo	to quarrel	13
抓	抓	zhuā	to catch	13
改	改	gǎi	to change	13
否	否	fǒu	no	14
忍	忍	rěn	to endure	14
汪	汪	wāng	(of liquid) collect	14
求	求	qiú	to beg	15
均	均	jūn	equal	18
即	即	jí	namely	20
免	免	miǎn	to avoid	20
攻	攻	gōng	to study, attact	20

8

表	表	biǎo	表演: to perform, play	2
拉	拉	lā	to play (certain musical instruments)	2
長	长	cháng	long	2
往	往	wǎng	to, towards	3
降	降	jiàng	to fall, lower	3
拐	拐	guǎi	to turn	3
直	直	zhí	straight	3
花	花	huā	(of eyes) blurred	4
味	味	wèi	taste	4
於	于	yú	終於: at last	5
取	取	qǔ	to take, withdraw	6
金	金	jīn	gold	6
抽	抽	chōu	to extract	7
宜	宜	yí	suitable	7
季	季	jì	season	7
果	果	guǒ	fruit; result	7
肥	肥	féi	fat	9
怪	怪	guài	strange	9
制	制	zhì	to control	9
注	注	zhù	to concentrate	9
受	受	shòu	to receive	10
爬	爬	pá	to climb	10
底	底	dǐ	bottom	11
拖	拖	tuō	to delay	11
況	况	kuàng	situation	11
性	性	xìng	nature (used as a suffix)	11
盲	盲	máng	blind	11

炎	炎	yán	inflammation	11
怕	怕	pà	to fear	11
幸	幸	xìng	luck	12
建	建	jiàn	to establish	13
使	使	shǐ	to make, cause	13
肩	肩	jiān	shoulder	13
抱	抱	bào	to hold, embrace	13
易	易	yì	easy	13
委	委	wěi	to appoint	14
屈	屈	qū	to bend	14
帖	帖	tiě	card note	15
佩	佩	pèi	to admire	16
油	油	yóu	oil, gasoline	16
拒	拒	jù	to reject	17
招	招	zhāo	to attract, recruit	17
供	供	gòng	to supply	18
争	争	zhēng	to contend	19
股	股	gǔ	section	19
固	固	gù	solid	19

9

負	负	fù	to bear	1
咱	咱	zán	we (including both the speaker and the person/s spoken to)	1
胡	胡	hú	barbarian, (胡琴: two-string bow instrument)	2
奏	奏	zòu	to play (a musical instrument), pluck	2
神	神	shén	spirit	2
計	计	jì	to count, calculate	3
品	品	pǐn	article, product	3
香	香	xiāng	aroma, good smell	4
便	便	biàn	convenient	4
相	相	xiāng	mutually	4
津	津	jīn	saliva	5
界	界	jiè	boundary	5
挺	挺	tǐng	very, quite	5
訂	订	dìng	to book, order	7
拜	拜	bài	to make a courtesy call	7
查	查	chá	to check, investigate, consult	7

故	故	gù	reason, old	8
持	持	chí	to keep, maintain	9
苗	苗	miáo	苗條: slim	9
孩	孩	hái	child	9
食	食	shí	food	9
急	急	jí	urgent	11
恢	恢	huī	extensive	12
段	段	duàn	section, segment	12
待	待	dāi	to stay	12
哎	哎	āi	(interjection)	12
俗	俗	sú	common	12
架	架	jià	to fight	13
退	退	tuì	to return	13
怨	怨	yuàn	to complain	13
封	封	fēng	(measure word for letters)	14
既	既	jì	as well as	14
音	音	yīn	sound	14
卻	却	què	but	15
括	括	kuò	to include	16
首	首	shǒu	head, first	17
突	突	tū	sticking out	17
限	限	xiàn	to limit, restrict	17
科	科	kē	section, science	18
咨	咨	zī	to consult	18
洽	洽	qià	to fit, suit	19
挑	挑	tiāo	to pick, select	20

10

倒	倒	dào	to move backward	1
破	破	pò	broken	1
套	套	tào	cover	1
拿	拿	ná	to hold	2
座	座	zuò	seat	2
站	站	zhàn	to stand	2
乘	乘	chéng	to take (a ship, plane, etc.)	3
航	航	háng	to navigate	3
展	展	zhǎn	to stretch	3
素	素	sù	basic element	4
特	特	tè	specially	4
差	差	chāi	errand, job	4
俱	俱	jù	all, completely	4
陰	阴	yīn	overcast	5
笑	笑	xiào	to laugh	5

琴	琴	qín	a general name mostly for string instruments	2
畫	画	huà	to draw, paint	2
棟	栋	dòng	(measure word for buildings)	3
喔	喔	ō	(an interjection indicating sudden realization)	3
費	费	fèi	cost, expenditure	3
睏	困	kùn	sleepy	4
街	街	jiē	street	4
款	款	kuǎn	a sum of money	6
單	单	dān	single; bill	6
換	换	huàn	to exchange	6
寒	寒	hán	cold	7
遊	游	yóu	to wander about	7
報	报	bào	to announce	8
描	描	miáo	to copy, retouch	8
越	越	yuè	to exceed	9
減	减	jiǎn	to reduce	9
飲	饮	yǐn	drink	9
超	超	chāo	to exceed	9
訴	诉	sù	to tell	10
診	诊	zhěn	to examine	11
順	顺	shùn	smooth	11
結	结	jié	tie	11
答	答	dá	to reply	12
煮	煮	zhǔ	to cook	12
跑	跑	pǎo	to run	12
悶	闷	mēn	to bore	12
堪	堪	kān	to bear, endure	12
補	补	bǔ	to repair	12
逼	逼	bī	to force	13
脾	脾	pí	spleen	13
遇	遇	yù	to meet	15
絞	绞	jiǎo	to wring	15
遍	遍	biàn	all over	15
趁	趁	chèn	to avail oneself of	16
提	提	tí	to refer to; carry	16
無	无	wú	without	16
量	量	liàng	measure	16
絡	络	luò	to wrap around; a net	15

番	番	fān	(measure word for cause)	16
絕	绝	jué	absolutely	17
曾	曾	céng	ever	18
項	项	xiàng	item, term	18
賀	贺	hè	to congratulate	19
虛	虚	xū	void, humble	19
貼	贴	tiē	補貼: allowance	19
猶	犹	yóu	still	19

13

裝	装	zhuāng	to install; clothes	1
照	照	zhào	to take (pictures)	2
鼓	鼓	gǔ	drum	2
落	落	luò	to drop, land	3
搭	搭	dā	to take (a ship, plane, etc.)	3
農	农	nóng	agriculture	3
睛	睛	jīng	eyeball	4
飽	饱	bǎo	to be full	4
廈	厦	shà	tall building	5
填	填	tián	to fill in	6
當	当	dāng	當然: of course	6
匯	汇	huì	collection	6
羨	羡	xiàn	to admire, envy	7
概	概	gài	general	7
節	节	jié	part; festival	8
矮	矮	ǎi	short	9
零	零	líng	zero	10
載	载	zài	to carry, be loaded with	10
腸	肠	cháng	intestines	11
頓	顿	dùn	(measure word for meals or scolds)	11
解	解	jiě	to solve	12
亂	乱	luàn	in a mess	12
煩	烦	fán	to bother	12
楣	霉	méi	倒楣: bad luck	12
催	催	cuī	to urge	13
搞	搞	gǎo	to do	13
禍	祸	huò	misfortune, disaster	13
塞	塞	sāi	to fill in	13
禁	禁	jìn	to prohibit	13

警	警	jǐng	to alert	13
寶	宝	bǎo	treasure	16
繼	继	jì	to continue	16
響	响	xiǎng	sound, ring	16
競	竞	jìng	to compete	19

21

顧	顾	gù	to look, consider	11
護	护	hù	to protect	11
續	续	xù	to continue	16

22

彎	弯	wān	curve	3
讀	读	dú	to read, study	16
驗	验	yàn	to examine	16

23

| 變 | 变 | biàn | to change | 3 |
| 顯 | 显 | xiǎn | to display | 14 |

24

| 靈 | 灵 | líng | quick, clever | 9 |

写字簿生字索引–简体字 CHARACTER BOOK INDEX – SIMPLIFIED CHARACTER VERSION (BY NUMBER OF STROKES)

Each entry lists simplified character, traditional character, Pinyin, English meaning, and lesson number:

		shè	agency, society	7
社	社	zhèng	certificate	7
证	證	bào	to announce	8
报	報	gào	to notify, announce	8
告	告	wán	finish, complete	8
完	完	jì	skill	8
技	技	jiān	hard, firm	9
坚	堅	yǐn	drink	9
饮	飲	chǐ	(a unit of length) foot	9
呀	呀	líng	quick, clever	9
灵	靈	gèng	even, more	9
更	更	xī	to hope	10
希	希	zhù	to aid, help	10
助	助	sù	to tell	10
诉	訴	zhé	to bend, twist	10
折	折	dù	belly	11
肚	肚	kuàng	situation	11
况	況	hù	to protect	11
护	護	zhěn	to examine	11
诊	診	cháng	intestines	11
肠	腸	shù	to bind	11
束	束	luàn	in a mess	12
乱	亂	mēn	to bore	12
闷	悶	hé	why not	12
何	何	chū	at the beginning of	12
初	初	bǔ	to repair	12
补	補	chǎo	to quarrel	13
吵	吵	zhuā	to catch	13
抓	抓	chí	late	13
迟	遲	shēng	sound	13
声	聲	gǎi	to change	13
改	改	fǒu	no	14
否	否	lì	(onomatopoeia)	14
沥	瀝	gōu	channel, ditch	14
沟	溝	rěn	to endure	14
忍	忍	wāng	(of liquid) collect	14
汪	汪	qiú	to beg	15
求	求	què	but	15
却	卻	rǎo	to harass, trouble	16
扰	擾	jù	to reject	17
拒	拒	jūn	equal	18
均	均	liáo	to cure, treat	19
疗	療	jí	namely	20
即	即	miǎn	to avoid	20
免	免	gōng	to study, attact	20
攻	攻			

8

		zé	duty	1
责	責	biǎo	表演: to perform, play	2
表	表	lā	to play (certain musical instruments)	2
拉	拉	huà	to draw, paint	2
画	畫	wǎng	to, towards	3
往	往	jiàng	to fall, lower	3
降	降	guǎi	to turn	3
拐	拐	zhí	straight	3
直	直	biàn	to change	3
变	變	zhuǎn	to turn	3
转	轉	fà	hair	4
发	髮	wèi	taste	4
味	味	bǎo	to be full	4
饱	飽	zhōng	end	5
终	終	nào	to do, make	5
闹	鬧	zhàng	account	6
账	帳	qǔ	to take, withdraw	6
取	取	dān	single; bill	6
单	單	jīn	gold	6
金	金	guì	cabinet	6
柜	櫃	chōu	to extract	7
抽	抽	yí	suitable	7
宜	宜	jì	season	7
季	季	guǒ	fruit; result	7
果	果	sōng	loose, slack	8
松	鬆	zhōu	week; circuit	8
周	週	féi	fat	9
肥	肥	guài	strange	9
怪	怪	miáo	苗条: slim	9
苗	苗	zhì	to control	9
制	制	zhù	to concentrate	9
注	注	shòu	to receive	10
受	受	pá	to climb	10
爬	爬	dǐng	summit	10
顶	頂	dǐ	bottom	11
底	底	tuō	to delay	11
拖	拖	xìng	nature (used as a suffix)	11
性	性			
		máng	blind	11
盲	盲	yán	inflammation	11
炎	炎	dān	to undertake	11
担	擔			

怕	怕	pà	to fear	11
怜	憐	lián	to pity	11
哎	哎	āi	(interjection)	12
幸	幸	xìng	luck	12
建	建	jiàn	to establish	13
货	貨	huò	goods	13
使	使	shǐ	to make, cause	13
肩	肩	jiān	shoulder	13
抱	抱	bào	to hold, embrace	13
易	易	yì	easy	13
委	委	wěi	to appoint	14
屈	屈	qū	to bend	14
泪	淚	lèi	tear	14
录	錄	lù	to record	15
购	購	gòu	to purchase	15
帖	帖	tiě	card note	15
宝	寶	bǎo	treasure	16
佩	佩	pèi	to admire	16
油	油	yóu	oil, gasoline	16
质	質	zhì	quality, nature	17
细	細	xì	thin, fine	17
招	招	zhāo	to attract, recruit	17
限	限	xiàn	to limit, restrict	17
询	詢	xún	to inquire	18
软	軟	ruǎn	soft	18
供	供	gòng	to supply	18
组	組	zǔ	group	18
织	織	zhī	to knit	18
股	股	gǔ	section	19
固	固	gù	solid	19
环	環	huán	annulus, loop	19
奋	奮	fèn	to act vigorouly	20

9

树	樹	shù	tree	1
挂	掛	guà	to hang	1
咱	咱	zán	we (including both the speaker and the person/s spoken to)	1
种	種	zhǒng	kind, type	2
胡	胡	hú	barbarian, (胡琴: two-string bow instrument)	2

奏	奏	zòu	to play (a musical instrument), pluck	2
神	神	shén	spirit	2
品	品	pǐn	article, product	3
栋	棟	dòng	(measure word for buildings)	3
弯	彎	wān	curve	3
费	費	fèi	cost, expenditure	3
轻	輕	qīng	small in degree	4
适	適	shì	fit, suitable	4
香	香	xiāng	aroma, good smell	4
便	便	biàn	convenient	4
相	相	xiāng	mutually	4
误	誤	wù	to miss	5
津	津	jīn	saliva	5
界	界	jiè	boundary	5
荣	榮	róng	glory	5
虽	雖	suī	although	5
挺	挺	tǐng	very, quite	5
亲	親	qīn	relative	7
拜	拜	bài	to make a courtesy call	7
查	查	chá	to check, investigate, consult	7
故	故	gù	reason, old	8
持	持	chí	to keep, maintain	9
孩	孩	hái	child	9
食	食	shí	food	9
总	總	zǒng	all, general	9
急	急	jí	urgent	11
顺	順	shùn	smooth	11
养	養	yǎng	to raise	11
结	結	jié	tie	11
骂	罵	mà	to scold	11
恢	恢	huī	extensive	12
段	段	duàn	section, segment	12
待	待	dāi	to stay	12
险	險	xiǎn	danger	12
俗	俗	sú	common	12
架	架	jià	to fight	13
退	退	tuì	to return	13
罚	罰	fá	to punish	13
怨	怨	yuàn	to complain	13
封	封	fēng	(measure word for letters)	14

显	顯	xiǎn	to display	14
既	既	jì	as well as	14
音	音	yīn	sound	14
络	絡	luò	to wrap around; a net	15
绞	絞	jiǎo	to wring	15
响	響	xiǎng	sound, ring	16
括	括	kuò	to include	16
济	濟	jì	to aid, help	16
将	將	jiāng	to support	16
奖	獎	jiǎng	award	16
复	複	fù	complex, complicated	17
首	首	shǒu	head, first	17
突	突	tū	sticking out	17
绝	絕	jué	absolutely	17
修	修	xiū	to repair, trim	17
荐	薦	jiàn	to recommend	17
科	科	kē	section, science	18
咨	咨	zī	to consult	18
除	除	chú	except	18
项	項	xiàng	item, term	18
贺	賀	hè	to congratulate	19
贴	貼	tiē	补贴: allowance	19
洽	洽	qià	to fit, suit	19
挑	挑	tiāo	to pick, select	20
选	選	xuǎn	to select	20
获	獲	huò	to win, obtain	20
标	標	biāo	mark	20

10

倒	倒	dào	to move backward	1
破	破	pò	broken	1
套	套	tào	cover	1
拿	拿	ná	to hold	2
座	座	zuò	seat	2
站	站	zhàn	to stand	2
乘	乘	chéng	to take (a ship, plane, etc.)	3
航	航	háng	to navigate	3
展	展	zhǎn	to stretch	3
素	素	sù	basic element	4
特	特	tè	specially	4
凉	凉	liáng	cool, cold	4

差	差	chāi	errand, job	4
俱	俱	jù	all, completely	4
赶	趕	gǎn	to catch, take	5
笑	笑	xiào	to laugh	5
值	值	zhí	to be worth	5
换	換	huàn	to exchange	6
原	原	yuán	primary, original	7
效	效	xiào	effect	8
根	根	gēn	root, base	10
载	載	zài	to carry, be loaded with	10
被	被	bèi	by	11
顾	顧	gù	to look, consider	11
唉	唉	āi	(interjection)	11
害	害	hài	to harm	11
通	通	tōng	through, connect	11
紧	緊	jǐn	tight	11
顿	頓	dùn	(measure word for meals or scolds)	11
恭	恭	gōng	to respect	12
悔	悔	huǐ	to regret	12
烦	煩	fán	to bother	12
缺	缺	quē	to lack	12
席	席	xí	seat	12
谊	誼	yì	friendship	12
谈	談	tán	to chat, talk	13
陪	陪	péi	to accompany	13
速	速	sù	speed	13
容	容	róng	to hold	13
谅	諒	liàng	to forgive	13
哭	哭	kū	to weep	14
流	流	liú	flow, current	15
索	索	suǒ	to search	15
铃	鈴	líng	bell	16
继	繼	jì	to continue	16
读	讀	dú	to read, study	16
途	途	tú	road, route	16
验	驗	yàn	to examine	16
调	調	tiáo	to adjust	17
格	格	gé	case	17
恐	恐	kǒng	to fear	17
虑	慮	lǜ	to consider	17
竞	競	jìng	to compete	19
资	資	zī	expense, money	19

谦	謙	qiān	modest	19
确	確	què	truly, firmly	19

13

照	照	zhào	to take (pictures)	2
摆	擺	bǎi	to put, place	2
鼓	鼓	gǔ	drum	2
满	滿	mǎn	full	2
睛	睛	jīng	eyeball	4
蓄	蓄	xù	to save up	6
填	填	tián	to fill in	6
数	數	shù	number	7
签	簽	qiān	to sign, label	7
概	概	gài	general	7
矮	矮	ǎi	short	9
零	零	líng	zero	10
解	解	jiě	to solve	12
催	催	cuī	to urge	13
搞	搞	gǎo	to do	13
塞	塞	sāi	to fill in	13
禁	禁	jìn	to prohibit	13
跳	跳	tiào	to jump	14
楚	楚	chǔ	thistle	14
简	簡	jiǎn	brief	17
聘	聘	pìn	to engage, hire	17
福	福	fú	blessing, goof fortune	19

14

墙	牆	qiáng	wall	2
演	演	yǎn	to perform, play	2
算	算	suàn	to plan, calculate	3
精	精	jīng	energy, spirit	4
聚	聚	jù	to gather	4
需	需	xū	need	9
瘦	瘦	shòu	thin	9
管	管	guǎn	to care	11
霉	楣	méi	倒霉: bad luck	12
察	察	chá	to check	13
歉	歉	qiàn	apology	13
滴	滴	dī	drop	14
磁	磁	cí	magnet	15
碟	碟	dié	disc	15

歌	歌	gē	song	15
愿	願	yuàn	to desire, wish	17
嘉	嘉	jiā	to praise	18
稳	穩	wěn	stable, steady	19
境	境	jìng	area, condition	19
赚	賺	zhuàn	to make profit	19

15

撞	撞	zhuàng	to collide	1
箱	箱	xiāng	box, case	1
慕	慕	mù	to admire, yarn for	7
趣	趣	qù	interest	8
颜	顏	yán	color	8
磅	磅	bàng	pound	9
躺	躺	tǎng	to lie, recline	12
趟	趟	tàng	(measure word for trips)	12
靠	靠	kào	to depend	12
瞒	瞞	mán	to hide the truth from	14
劈	劈	pī	to split; (onomatopoeia)	14
懂	懂	dǒng	to understand	16
聪	聰	cōng	acute hearing	17
豫	豫	yù	to comfort, to please	19

16

镜	鏡	jìng	mirror	1
整	整	zhěng	to put in order	1
器	器	qì	utensil, ware	2
磨	磨	mó	to grind	16
融	融	róng	to melt	19
薪	薪	xīn	salary	19

17

繁	繁	fán	numerous, grand	5
糟	糟	zāo	bad	12

19

簿	簿	bù	book	6
警	警	jǐng	to alert	13

Each entry lists traditional character, simplified character, Pinyin, and English meaning:

Lesson 1

倒	倒	dào	to move backward
別	别	bié	don't
樹	树	shù	tree
撞	撞	zhuàng	to collide
壞	坏	huài	bad
呀	呀	ya	(indicating surprise)
鏡	镜	jìng	mirror
破	破	pò	broken
合	合	hé	to combine
主	主	zhǔ	主意: idea
負	负	fù	to bear
責	责	zé	duty
李	李	lǐ	行李: luggage
裝	装	zhuāng	to install; clothes
掃	扫	sǎo	to sweep
整	整	zhěng	to put in order
理	理	lǐ	to put in order
箱	箱	xiāng	box, case
衣	衣	yī	clothes
掛	挂	guà	to hang
累	累	lèi	tired
死	死	sǐ	dead
附	附	fù	be near
忘	忘	wàng	to forget
窗	窗	chuāng	window
套	套	tào	cover
咱	咱	zán	we (including both the speaker and the person/s spoken to)

Lesson 2

牆	墙	qiáng	wall
著	着	zhe	(a particle indicating an aspect)
照	照	zhào	to take (pictures)

片	片	piàn	thin piece
北	北	běi	north
台	台	tái	stage, platform
擺	摆	bǎi	to put, place
各	各	gè	each, every
種	种	zhǒng	kind, type
器	器	qì	utensil, ware
演	演	yǎn	to perform, play
表	表	biǎo	表演: to perform, play
鼓	鼓	gǔ	drum
拉	拉	lā	to play (certain musical instruments)
胡	胡	hú	barbarian, (胡琴: two-string bow instrument)
琴	琴	qín	a general name mostly for string instruments
彈	弹	tán	to play (a musical instrument), pluck
奏	奏	zòu	to play (a musical instrument)
己	己	jǐ	oneself
齣	出	chū	(measure word for dramas)
戲	戏	xì	traditional Chinese opera
畫	画	huà	to draw, paint
臉	脸	liǎn	face
拿	拿	ná	to hold
刀	刀	dāo	knife
神	神	shén	spirit
座	座	zuò	seat
滿	满	mǎn	full
眾	众	zhòng	multitude
站	站	zhàn	to stand
長	长	cháng	long

Lesson 3

往	往	wǎng	to, towards
降	降	jiàng	to fall, lower
落	落	luò	to drop, land
全	全	quán	whole; intact
繫	系	jì	to fasten
計	计	jì	to count, calculate
算	算	suàn	to plan, calculate
品	品	pǐn	article, product
搭	搭	dā	to take (a ship, plane, etc.)
乘	乘	chéng	to take (a ship, plane, etc.)
航	航	háng	to navigate
棟	栋	dòng	(measure word for buildings)
交	交	jiāo	(of places or periods of time) meet, join
叉	叉	chā	cross
口	口	kǒu	mouth, entrance
左	左	zuǒ	left
拐	拐	guǎi	to turn
直	直	zhí	straight
里	里	lǐ	公里: kilometer
展	展	zhǎn	to stretch
變	变	biàn	to change
化	化	huà	變(变)化: change
農	农	nóng	agriculture
田	田	tián	field
成	成	chéng	to become
喔	喔	ō	(an interjection indicating sudden realization)
尺	尺	chǐ	ruler
山	山	shān	mountain
燈	灯	dēng	light, lamp
向	向	xiàng	to, towards
右	右	yòu	right
轉	转	zhuǎn	to turn
彎	弯	wān	curve
費	费	fèi	cost, expenditure
民	民	mín	people
幣	币	bì	money, currency

Lesson 4

母	母	mǔ	mother
維	维	wéi	to maintain
素	素	sù	basic element
永	永	yǒng	forever
康	康	kāng	healthy
輕	轻	qīng	small in degree
特	特	tè	specially
涼	凉	liáng	cool, cold
精	精	jīng	energy, spirit
髮	发	fà	hair
眼	眼	yǎn	eye
睛	睛	jīng	eyeball
花	花	huā	(of eyes) blurred
適	适	shì	fit, suitable
差	差	chāi	errand, job
睏	困	kùn	sleepy
街	街	jiē	street
慣	惯	guàn	to be in the habit of
味	味	wèi	taste
香	香	xiāng	aroma, good smell
俱	俱	jù	all, completely
飽	饱	bǎo	to be full
便	便	biàn	convenient
相	相	xiāng	mutually
聚	聚	jù	to gather
乾	干	gān	dry; to empty
亦	亦	yì	also
乎	乎	hū	(a particle expressing doubt or conjecture)

Lesson 5

陰	阴	yīn	overcast
終	终	zhōng	end
於	于	yú	終於(终于): at last
誤	误	wù	to miss
趕	赶	gǎn	to catch, take
情	情	qíng	affection
津	津	jīn	saliva
界	界	jiè	boundary
團	团	tuán	group
鬧	闹	nào	to do, make
笑	笑	xiào	to laugh

繁榮廈雖挺值	繁荣厦虽挺值	fán	numerous, grand
		róng	glory
		shà	tall building
		suī	although
		tǐng	very, quite
		zhí	to be worth

Lesson 6

銀帳戶存款取利率儲蓄之支職低夠單填千元金寄簿卡當換匯兌櫃	银账户存款取利率储蓄之支职低够单填千元金寄簿卡当换汇兑柜	yín	silver
		zhàng	account
		hù	door; (bank) account
		cún	to deposit
		kuǎn	a sum of money
		qǔ	to take, withdraw
		lì	profit, interest
		lǜ	rate
		chǔ	to store up
		xù	to save up
		zhī	(a particle)
		zhī	to pay out; withdraw
		zhí	duty
		dī	low
		gòu	sufficient
		dān	single; bill
		tián	to fill in
		qiān	thousand
		yuán	dollar
		jīn	gold
		jì	to mail, send
		bù	book
		kǎ	card
		dāng	當(当)然: of course
		huàn	to exchange
		huì	collection
		duì	to exchange
		guì	cabinet

Lesson 7

寒遊社訂羨	寒游社订羨	hán	cold
		yóu	to wander about
		shè	agency, society
		dìng	to book, order
		xiàn	to admire, envy

慕親戚原抽拜	慕亲戚原抽拜	mù	to admire, yarn for
		qīn	relative
		qī	relative
		yuán	primary, original
		chōu	to extract
		bài	to make a courtesy call
訪查	访查	fǎng	to visit
		chá	to check, investigate, consult
宜季數族果簽證辦概及	宜季数族果签证办概及	yí	suitable
		jì	season
		shù	number
		zú	nationality
		guǒ	fruit; result
		qiān	to sign, label
		zhèng	certificate
		bàn	to handle
		gài	general
		jí	to reach, attain

Lesson 8

連報告鬆強完導夫它節引古代故彩描歷史趣而且	连报告松强完导夫它节引古代故彩描历史趣而且	lián	even
		bào	to announce
		gào	to notify, announce
		sōng	loose, slack
		qiáng	strong; better
		wán	finish, complete
		dǎo	to lead, guide
		fū	功夫: Kung Fu
		tā	it
		jié	part; festival
		yǐn	to lead, attract
		gǔ	ancient
		dài	historical period; generation
		gù	reason, old
		cǎi	color; variety
		miáo	to copy, retouch
		lì	to go through
		shǐ	history
		qù	interest
		ér	而且: also, in addition
		qiě	而且: also, in addition

技	技	jì	skill
效	效	xiào	effect
顏	颜	yán	color
週	周	zhōu	week; circuit
末	末	mò	end
價	价	jià	price, value

Lesson 9

越	越	yuè	to exceed
需	需	xū	need
瘦	瘦	shòu	thin
減	减	jiǎn	to reduce
肥	肥	féi	fat
堅	坚	jiān	hard, firm
持	持	chí	to keep, maintain
磅	磅	bàng	pound
怪	怪	guài	strange
苗	苗	miáo	苗條(条): slim
孩	孩	hái	child
控	控	kòng	to control
制	制	zhì	to control
飲	饮	yǐn	drink
食	食	shí	food
注	注	zhù	to concentrate
甜	甜	tián	sweet
早	早	zǎo	early
矮	矮	ǎi	short
呎	呎	chǐ	(a unit of length) foot
吋	吋	cùn	inch
超	超	chāo	to exceed
靈	灵	líng	quick, clever
總	总	zǒng	all, general
更	更	gèng	even, more

Lesson 10

希	希	xī	to hope
望	望	wàng	to hope
旬	旬	xún	a period of ten days
受	受	shòu	to receive
商	商	shāng	trade, business
根	根	gēn	root, base
據	据	jù	to depend on

零	零	líng	zero
爬	爬	pá	to climb
頂	顶	dǐng	summit
助	助	zhù	to aid, help
漢	汉	hàn	man
訴	诉	sù	to tell
壯	壮	zhuàng	strong; grand
曲	曲	qū	bend, crooked
折	折	zhé	to bend, twist
載	载	zài	to carry, be loaded with
歸	归	guī	to return

Lesson 11

被	被	bèi	by
顧	顾	gù	to look, consider
底	底	dǐ	bottom
唉	唉	āi	(interjection)
肚	肚	dù	belly
管	管	guǎn	to care
拖	拖	tuō	to delay
厲	厉	lì	severe
害	害	hài	to harm
剛	刚	gāng	just
況	况	kuàng	situation
救	救	jiù	to rescue
護	护	hù	to protect
急	急	jí	urgent
診	诊	zhěn	to examine
性	性	xìng	nature (used as a suffix)
盲	盲	máng	blind
腸	肠	cháng	intestines
炎	炎	yán	inflammation
術	术	shù	skill, technigue
嚇	吓	xià	to scare
擔	担	dān	to undertake
順	顺	shùn	smooth
士	士	shì	person
推	推	tuī	to push
養	养	yǎng	to raise
通	通	tōng	through, connect
怕	怕	pà	to fear
敢	敢	gǎn	to dare

結	结	jié	tie
束	束	shù	to bind
緊	紧	jǐn	tight
罵	骂	mà	to scold
頓	顿	dùn	(measure word for meals or scolds)
憐	怜	lián	to pity
父	父	fù	father

Lesson 12

由	由	yóu	from
解	解	jiě	to solve
答	答	dá	to reply
煮	煮	zhǔ	to cook
恭	恭	gōng	to respect
恢	恢	huī	extensive
啦	啦	la	(particle)
段	段	duàn	section, segment
亂	乱	luàn	in a mess
跑	跑	pǎo	to run
待	待	dāi	to stay
躺	躺	tǎng	to lie, recline
悶	闷	mēn	to bore
此	此	cǐ	this
何	何	hé	why not
初	初	chū	at the beginning of
檢	检	jiǎn	to examine
哎	哎	āi	(interjection)
悔	悔	huǐ	to regret
虧	亏	kuī	fortunately; to lose
糟	糟	zāo	bad
幸	幸	xìng	luck
堪	堪	kān	to bear, endure
設	设	shè	to establish
趙	趟	tàng	(measure word for trips)
麻	麻	má	hemp
煩	烦	fán	to bother
險	险	xiǎn	danger
缺	缺	quē	to lack
席	席	xí	seat
輔	辅	fǔ	to assist
補	补	bǔ	to repair

至	至	zhì	to reach
楣	霉	méi	倒楣(霉): bad luck
俗	俗	sú	common
靠	靠	kào	to depend
誼	谊	yì	friendship

Lesson 13

催	催	cuī	to urge
吵	吵	chǎo	to quarrel
架	架	jià	to fight
談	谈	tán	to chat, talk
建	建	jiàn	to establish
議	议	yì	to discuss
搞	搞	gǎo	to do
又	又	yòu	again
退	退	tuì	to return
貨	货	huò	goods
陪	陪	péi	to accompany
專	专	zhuān	to concentrate
速	速	sù	speed
禍	祸	huò	misfortune, disaster
塞	塞	sāi	to fill in
禁	禁	jìn	to prohibit
止	止	zhǐ	to stop
使	使	shǐ	to make, cause
匆	匆	cōng	hurriedly
逼	逼	bī	to force
肩	肩	jiān	shoulder
警	警	jǐng	to alert
察	察	chá	to check
抓	抓	zhuā	to catch
罰	罚	fá	to punish
遲	迟	chí	late
聲	声	shēng	sound
抱	抱	bào	to hold, embrace
怨	怨	yuàn	to complain
守	守	shǒu	to guard
脾	脾	pí	spleen
容	容	róng	to hold
易	易	yì	easy
改	改	gǎi	to change
歉	歉	qiàn	apology
諒	谅	liàng	to forgive

Lesson 14

撲	扑	pū	to throw oneself on
跳	跳	tiào	to jump
封	封	fēng	(measure word for letters)
顯	显	xiǎn	to display
示	示	shì	to notify, show
聊	聊	liáo	to chat
否	否	fǒu	no
淅	淅	xī	(onomatopoeia)
瀝	沥	lì	(onomatopoeia)
溝	沟	gōu	channel, ditch
滴	滴	dī	drop
忍	忍	rěn	to endure
傷	伤	shāng	wound
失	失	shī	to lose
哭	哭	kū	to weep
委	委	wěi	to appoint
屈	屈	qū	to bend
淚	泪	lèi	tear
汪	汪	wāng	(of liquid) collect
危	危	wēi	danger
既	既	jì	as well as
瞞	瞒	mán	to hide the truth from
清	清	qīng	clear
楚	楚	chǔ	thistle
劈	劈	pī	to split; (onomatopoeia)
啪	啪	pā	(onomatopoeia)
毛	毛	máo	hair
音	音	yīn	sound

Lesson 15

求	求	qiú	to beg
磁	磁	cí	magnet
聯	联	lián	to connect
絡	络	luò	to wrap around; a net
卻	却	què	but
遇	遇	yù	to meet
錄	录	lù	to record
絞	绞	jiǎo	to wring
力	力	lì	strength
反	反	fǎn	in reverse
遍	遍	biàn	all over
碟	碟	dié	disc

歌	歌	gē	song
流	流	liú	flow, current
搜	搜	sōu	to search
索	索	suǒ	to search
購	购	gòu	to purchase
帖	帖	tiě	card note

Lesson 16

級	级	jí	level
趁	趁	chèn	to avail oneself of
叮	叮	dīng	(onomatopoeia)
噹	当	dāng	(onomatopoeia)
鈴	铃	líng	bell
響	响	xiǎng	sound, ring
提	提	tí	to refer to; carry
括	括	kuò	to include
世	世	shì	world; life
寶	宝	bǎo	treasure
懂	懂	dǒng	to understand
佩	佩	pèi	to admire
齊	齐	qí	uniform
繼	继	jì	to continue
續	续	xù	to continue
讀	读	dú	to read, study
濟	济	jì	to aid, help
碩	硕	shuò	large
授	授	shòu	to teach
將	将	jiāng	to support
途	途	tú	road, route
無	无	wú	without
量	量	liàng	measure
獎	奖	jiǎng	award
講	讲	jiǎng	to speak
驗	验	yàn	to examine
磨	磨	mó	to grind
番	番	fān	(measure word for cause)
油	油	yóu	oil, gasoline
擾	扰	rǎo	to harass, trouble

Lesson 17

| 簡 | 简 | jiǎn | brief |
| 複 | 复 | fù | complex, complicated |

雜	杂	zá	miscellaneous
首	首	shǒu	head, first
質	质	zhì	quality, nature
調	调	tiáo	to adjust
突	突	tū	sticking out
拒	拒	jù	to reject
絕	绝	jué	absolutely
仔	仔	zǐ	small and fine
細	细	xì	thin, fine
修	修	xiū	to repair, trim
招	招	zhāo	to attract, recruit
聘	聘	pìn	to engage, hire
格	格	gé	case
薦	荐	jiàn	to recommend
恐	恐	kǒng	to fear
限	限	xiàn	to limit, restrict
慮	虑	lǜ	to consider
聰	聪	cōng	acute hearing
幹	干	gàn	to do, work
願	愿	yuàn	to desire, wish

Lesson 18

任	任	rèn	to appoint
科	科	kē	section, science
份	份	fèn	(measure word for jobs)
咨	咨	zī	to consult
詢	询	xún	to inquire
軟	软	ruǎn	soft
供	供	gòng	to supply
儘	尽	jǐn	despite
除	除	chú	except
副	副	fù	assistant
均	均	jūn	equal
績	绩	jì	achievement
曾	曾	céng	ever
嘉	嘉	jiā	to praise
組	组	zǔ	group
織	织	zhī	to knit
凡	凡	fán	every; ordinary
項	项	xiàng	item, term
目	目	mù	eye
論	论	lùn	to discuss

Lesson 19

寧	宁	nìng	寧願(宁愿): rather
融	融	róng	to melt
競	竞	jìng	to compete
爭	争	zhēng	to contend
賀	贺	hè	to congratulate
謙	谦	qiān	modest
虛	虚	xū	void, humble
資	资	zī	expense, money
穩	稳	wěn	stable, steady
薪	薪	xīn	salary
萬	万	wàn	ten thousand
股	股	gǔ	section
婆	婆	pó	mother-in-law, old woman
竟	竟	jìng	to complete, investigate
療	疗	liáo	to cure, treat
貼	贴	tiē	補貼(补贴): allowance
福	福	fú	blessing, goof fortune
猶	犹	yóu	still
豫	豫	yù	to comfort, to please
固	固	gù	solid
環	环	huán	annulus, loop
境	境	jìng	area, condition
確	确	què	truly, firmly
洽	洽	qià	to fit, suit
賺	赚	zhuàn	to make profit

Lesson 20

與	与	yǔ	與其(与其): rather than
即	即	jí	namely
奮	奋	fèn	to act vigorouly
挑	挑	tiāo	to pick, select
選	选	xuǎn	to select
謀	谋	móu	to plan, consult
免	免	miǎn	to avoid
獲	获	huò	to win, obtain
鬥	斗	dòu	to fight, to contest with
標	标	biāo	mark
攻	攻	gōng	to study, attact

寫字簿生字索引–拼音 CHARACTER BOOK INDEX (ALPHABETICAL BY PINYIN)

Each entry lists traditional character, simplified character, Pinyin, English meaning, and lesson number:

A

唉	唉	āi	(interjection)	11
哎	哎	āi	(interjection)	12
矮	矮	ǎi	short	9

B

擺	摆	bǎi	to put, place	2
拜	拜	bài	to make a courtesy call	7
辦	办	bàn	to handle	7
磅	磅	bàng	pound	9
飽	饱	bǎo	to be full	4
寶	宝	bǎo	treasure	16
報	报	bào	to announce	8
抱	抱	bào	to hold, embrace	13
北	北	běi	north	2
被	被	bèi	by	11
逼	逼	bī	to force	13
幣	币	bì	money, currency	3
變	变	biàn	to change	3
便	便	biàn	convenient	4
遍	遍	biàn	all over	15
標	标	biāo	mark	20
表	表	biǎo	表演: to perform, play	2
別	别	bié	don't	1
補	补	bǔ	to repair	12
簿	簿	bù	book	6

C

彩	彩	cǎi	color; variety	8
曾	曾	céng	ever	18
叉	叉	chā	cross	3
差	差	chāi	errand, job	4

查	查	chá	to check, investigate, consult	7
察	察	chá	to check	13
長	长	cháng	long	2
腸	肠	cháng	intestines	11
超	超	chāo	to exceed	9
吵	吵	chǎo	to quarrel	13
趁	趁	chèn	to avail oneself of	16
乘	乘	chéng	to take (a ship, plane, etc.)	3
成	成	chéng	to become	3
持	持	chí	to keep, maintain	9
遲	迟	chí	late	13
尺	尺	chǐ	ruler	3
呎	呎	chǐ	(a unit of length) foot	9
抽	抽	chōu	to extract	7
齣	出	chū	(measure word for dramas)	2
初	初	chū	at the beginning of	12
除	除	chú	except	18
儲	储	chǔ	to store up	6
楚	楚	chǔ	thistle	14
窗	窗	chuāng	window	1
磁	磁	cí	magnet	15
此	此	cǐ	this	12
匆	匆	cōng	hurriedly	13
聰	聪	cōng	acute hearing	17
催	催	cuī	to urge	13
存	存	cún	to deposit	6
吋	吋	cùn	inch	9

D

| 搭 | 搭 | dā | to take (a ship, plane, etc.) | 3 |
| 答 | 答 | dá | to reply | 12 |

待	待	dāi	to stay	12
代	代	dài	historical period; generation	8
單	单	dān	single; bill	6
擔	担	dān	to undertake	11
當	当	dāng	當(当)然: of course	6
噹	当	dāng	(onomatopoeia)	16
刀	刀	dāo	knife	2
導	导	dǎo	to lead, guide	8
倒	倒	dào	to move backward	1
燈	灯	dēng	light, lamp	3
低	低	dī	low	6
滴	滴	dī	drop	14
底	底	dǐ	bottom	11
碟	碟	dié	disc	15
叮	叮	dīng	(onomatopoeia)	16
頂	顶	dǐng	summit	10
訂	订	dìng	to book, order	7
懂	懂	dǒng	to understand	16
棟	栋	dòng	(measure word for buildings)	3
鬥	斗	dòu	to fight, to contest with	20
讀	读	dú	to read, study	16
肚	肚	dù	belly	11
段	段	duàn	section, segment	12
兌	兑	duì	to exchange	6
頓	顿	dùn	(measure word for meals or scolds)	11

E

| 而 | 而 | ér | 而且: also, in addition | 8 |

F

罰	罚	fá	to punish	13
髮	发	fà	hair	4
番	番	fān	(measure word for cause)	16
繁	繁	fán	numerous, grand	5
煩	烦	fán	to bother	12
凡	凡	fán	every; ordinary	18

反	反	fǎn	in reverse	15
訪	访	fǎng	to visit	7
肥	肥	féi	fat	9
費	费	fèi	cost, expenditure	3
份	份	fèn	(measure word for jobs)	18
奮	奋	fèn	to act vigorouly	20
封	封	fēng	(measure word for letters)	14
否	否	fǒu	no	14
夫	夫	fū	功夫: Kung Fu	8
福	福	fú	blessing, goof fortune	19
輔	辅	fǔ	to assist	12
負	负	fù	to bear	1
附	附	fù	be near	1
父	父	fù	father	11
複	复	fù	complex, complicated	17
副	副	fù	assistant	18

G

改	改	gǎi	to change	13
概	概	gài	general	7
乾	干	gān	dry; to empty	4
趕	赶	gǎn	to catch, take	5
敢	敢	gǎn	to dare	11
幹	干	gàn	to do, work	17
剛	刚	gāng	just	11
搞	搞	gǎo	to do	13
告	告	gào	to notify, announce	8
歌	歌	gē	song	15
格	格	gé	case	17
各	各	gè	each, every	2
根	根	gēn	root, base	10
更	更	gèng	even, more	9
恭	恭	gōng	to respect	12
攻	攻	gōng	to study, attact	20
供	供	gòng	to supply	18
溝	沟	gōu	channel, ditch	14
夠	够	gòu	sufficient	6
購	购	gòu	to purchase	15
古	古	gǔ	ancient	8
鼓	鼓	gǔ	drum	2

股	股	gǔ	section	19
故	故	gù	reason, old	8
顧	顾	gù	to look, consider	11
固	固	gù	solid	19
掛	挂	guà	to hang	1
拐	拐	guǎi	to turn	3
怪	怪	guài	strange	9
管	管	guǎn	to care	11
慣	惯	guàn	to be in the habit of	4
歸	归	guī	to return	10
櫃	柜	guì	cabinet	6
果	果	guǒ	fruit; result	7

H

孩	孩	hái	child	9
害	害	hài	to harm	11
寒	寒	hán	cold	7
漢	汉	hàn	man	10
航	航	háng	to navigate	3
合	合	hé	to combine	1
何	何	hé	why not	12
賀	贺	hè	to congratulate	19
乎	乎	hū	(a particle expressing doubt or conjecture)	4
胡	胡	hú	barbarian, (胡琴: two-string bow instrument)	2
戶	户	hù	door; (bank) account	6
護	护	hù	to protect	11
花	花	huā	(of eyes) blurred	4
畫	画	huà	to draw, paint	2
化	化	huà	變(变)化: change	3
壞	坏	huài	bad	1
環	环	huán	annulus, loop	19
換	换	huàn	to exchange	6
恢	恢	huī	extensive	12
悔	悔	huǐ	to regret	12
匯	汇	huì	collection	6
貨	货	huò	goods	13
禍	祸	huò	misfortune, disaster	13
獲	获	huò	to win, obtain	20

J

及	及	jí	to reach, attain	7
急	急	jí	urgent	11
級	级	jí	level	16
即	即	jí	namely	20
己	己	jǐ	oneself	2
繫	系	jì	to fasten	3
計	计	jì	to count, calculate	3
寄	寄	jì	to mail, send	6
季	季	jì	season	7
技	技	jì	skill	8
既	既	jì	as well as	14
繼	继	jì	to continue	16
濟	济	jì	to aid, help	16
績	绩	jì	achievement	18
嘉	嘉	jiā	to praise	18
價	价	jià	price, value	8
架	架	jià	to fight	13
堅	坚	jiān	hard, firm	9
肩	肩	jiān	shoulder	13
減	减	jiǎn	to reduce	9
檢	检	jiǎn	to examine	12
簡	简	jiǎn	brief	17
建	建	jiàn	to establish	13
薦	荐	jiàn	to recommend	17
將	将	jiāng	to support	16
獎	奖	jiǎng	award	16
講	讲	jiǎng	to speak	16
降	降	jiàng	to fall, lower	3
交	交	jiāo	(of places or periods of time) meet, join	3
絞	绞	jiǎo	to wring	15
街	街	jiē	street	4
節	节	jié	part; festival	8
結	结	jié	tie	11
解	解	jiě	to solve	12
界	界	jiè	boundary	5
津	津	jīn	saliva	5
金	金	jīn	gold	6
緊	紧	jǐn	tight	11
禁	禁	jìn	to prohibit	13
儘	尽	jǐn	despite	18
精	精	jīng	energy, spirit	4
睛	睛	jīng	eyeball	4

N

拿	拿	ná	to hold	2
鬧	闹	nào	to do, make	5
寧	宁	nìng	寧願(宁愿): rather	19
農	农	nóng	agriculture	3

O

喔	喔	ō	(an interjection indicating sudden realization)	3

P

啪	啪	pā	(onomatopoeia)	14
爬	爬	pá	to climb	10
怕	怕	pà	to fear	11
跑	跑	pǎo	to run	12
陪	陪	péi	to accompany	13
佩	佩	pèi	to admire	16
劈	劈	pī	to split; (onomatopoeia)	14
脾	脾	pí	spleen	13
片	片	piàn	thin piece	2
品	品	pǐn	article, product	3
聘	聘	pìn	to engage, hire	17
婆	婆	pó	mother-in-law, old woman	19
破	破	pò	broken	1
撲	扑	pū	to throw oneself on	14

Q

齊	齐	qí	uniform	16
戚	戚	qī	relative	7
器	器	qì	utensil, ware	2
洽	洽	qià	to fit, suit	19
千	千	qiān	thousand	6
簽	签	qiān	to sign, label	7
謙	谦	qiān	modest	19
歉	歉	qiàn	apology	13
牆	墙	qiáng	wall	2
強	强	qiáng	strong; better	8

且	且	qiě	而且: also, in addition	8
親	亲	qīn	relative	7
琴	琴	qín	a general name mostly for string instruments	2
輕	轻	qīng	small in degree	4
清	清	qīng	clear	14
情	情	qíng	affection	5
求	求	qiú	to beg	15
曲	曲	qū	bend, crooked	10
屈	屈	qū	to bend	14
取	取	qǔ	to take, withdraw	6
趣	趣	qù	interest	8
全	全	quán	whole; intact	3
缺	缺	quē	to lack	12
卻	却	què	but	15
確	确	què	truly, firmly	19

R

擾	扰	rǎo	to harass, trouble	16
忍	忍	rěn	to endure	14
任	任	rèn	to appoint	18
榮	荣	róng	glory	5
容	容	róng	to hold	13
融	融	róng	to melt	19
軟	软	ruǎn	soft	18

S

塞	塞	sāi	to fill in	13
掃	扫	sǎo	to sweep	1
廈	厦	shà	tall building	5
山	山	shān	mountain	3
商	商	shāng	trade, business	10
傷	伤	shāng	wound	14
社	社	shè	agency, society	7
設	设	shè	to establish	12
神	神	shén	spirit	2
聲	声	shēng	sound	13
失	失	shī	to lose	14
食	食	shí	food	9
史	史	shǐ	history	8
使	使	shǐ	to make, cause	13

相	相	xiāng	mutually	4
響	响	xiǎng	sound, ring	16
向	向	xiàng	to, towards	3
項	项	xiàng	item, term	18
笑	笑	xiào	to laugh	5
效	效	xiào	effect	8
薪	薪	xīn	salary	19
性	性	xìng	nature (used as a suffix)	11
幸	幸	xìng	luck	12
修	修	xiū	to repair, trim	17
需	需	xū	need	9
虛	虚	xū	void, humble	19
蓄	蓄	xù	to save up	6
續	续	xù	to continue	16
選	选	xuǎn	to select	20
旬	旬	xún	a period of ten days	10
詢	询	xún	to inquire	18

Y

呀	呀	ya	(indicating surprise)	1
顏	颜	yán	color	8
炎	炎	yán	inflammation	11
演	演	yǎn	to perform, play	2
眼	眼	yǎn	eye	4
驗	验	yàn	to examine	16
養	养	yǎng	to raise	11
衣	衣	yī	clothes	1
亦	亦	yì	also	4
宜	宜	yí	suitable	7
誼	谊	yì	friendship	12
議	议	yì	to discuss	13
易	易	yì	easy	13
陰	阴	yīn	overcast	5
音	音	yīn	sound	14
銀	银	yín	silver	6
引	引	yǐn	to lead, attract	8
飲	饮	yǐn	drink	9
永	永	yǒng	forever	4
遊	游	yóu	to wander about	7
由	由	yóu	from	12
油	油	yóu	oil, gasoline	16
猶	犹	yóu	still	19

右	右	yòu	right	3
又	又	yòu	again	13
於	于	yú	終於(终于): at last	5
與	与	yǔ	與其(与其): rather than	20
遇	遇	yù	to meet	15
豫	豫	yù	to comfort, to please	19
元	元	yuán	dollar	6
原	原	yuán	primary, original	7
怨	怨	yuàn	to complain	13
越	越	yuè	to exceed	9

Z

雜	杂	zá	miscellaneous	17
載	载	zài	to carry, be loaded with	10
咱	咱	zán	we (including both the speaker and the person/s spoken to)	1
糟	糟	zāo	bad	12
早	早	zǎo	early	9
責	责	zé	duty	1
展	展	zhǎn	to stretch	3
站	站	zhàn	to stand	2
帳	账	zhàng	account	6
招	招	zhāo	to attract, recruit	17
照	照	zhào	to take (pictures)	2
著	着	zhe	(a particle indicating an aspect)	2
折	折	zhé	to bend, twist	10
診	诊	zhěn	to examine	11
爭	争	zhēng	to contend	19
整	整	zhěng	to put in order	1
證	证	zhèng	certificate	7
之	之	zhī	(a particle)	6
支	支	zhī	to pay out; withdraw	6
織	织	zhī	to knit	18
職	职	zhí	duty	6
值	值	zhí	to be worth	5
直	直	zhí	straight	3
止	止	zhǐ	to stop	13
制	制	zhì	to control	9

至	至	zhì	to reach	12		裝	装	zhuāng	to install; clothes	1
質	质	zhì	quality, nature	17		撞	撞	zhuàng	to collide	1
終	终	zhōng	end	5		壯	壮	zhuàng	strong; grand	10
種	种	zhǒng	kind, type	2		咨	咨	zī	to consult	18
眾	众	zhòng	multitude	2		資	资	zī	expense, money	19
週	周	zhōu	week; circuit	8		仔	仔	zǐ	small and fine	17
主	主	zhǔ	主意: idea	1		總	总	zǒng	all, general	9
煮	煮	zhǔ	to cook	12		奏	奏	zòu	to play (a musical instrument), pluck	2
注	注	zhù	to concentrate	9						
助	助	zhù	to aid, help	10						
抓	抓	zhuā	to catch	13		族	族	zú	nationality	7
專	专	zhuān	to concentrate	13		組	组	zǔ	group	18
轉	转	zhuǎn	to turn	3		左	左	zuǒ	left	3
賺	赚	zhuàn	to make profit	19		座	座	zuò	seat	2

Name: _____ Date: _____

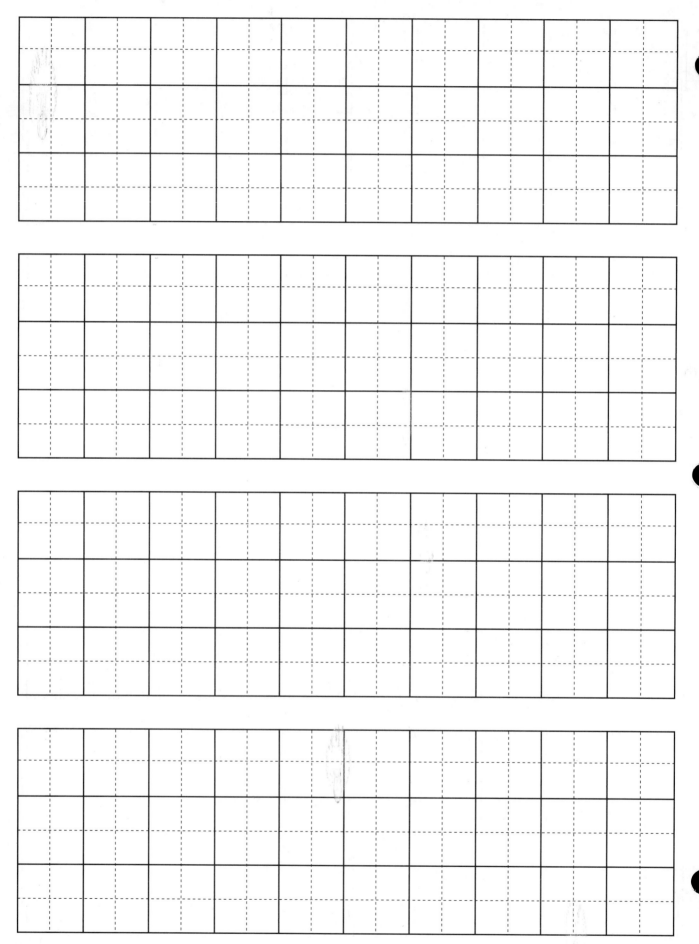

226

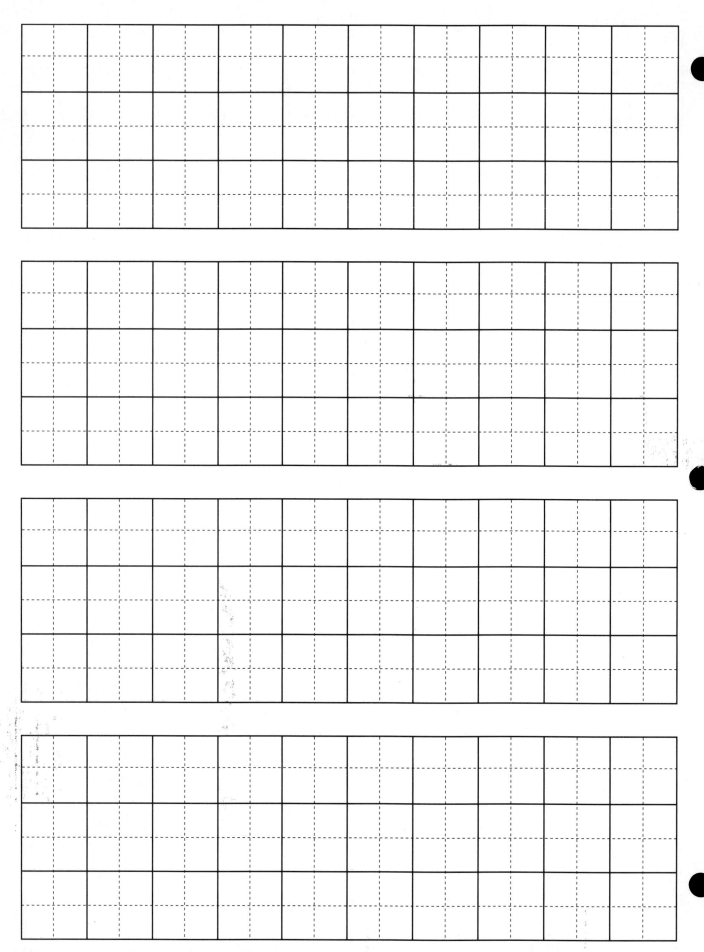

228

Name: _____ Date: _____

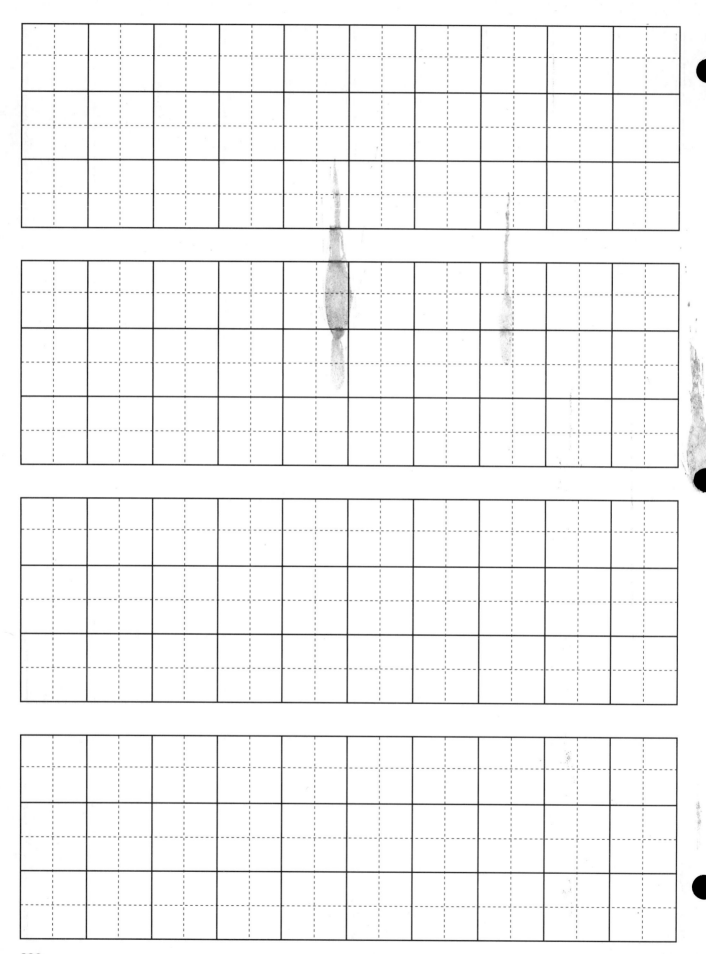

230

Name: _____ Date: _____

231

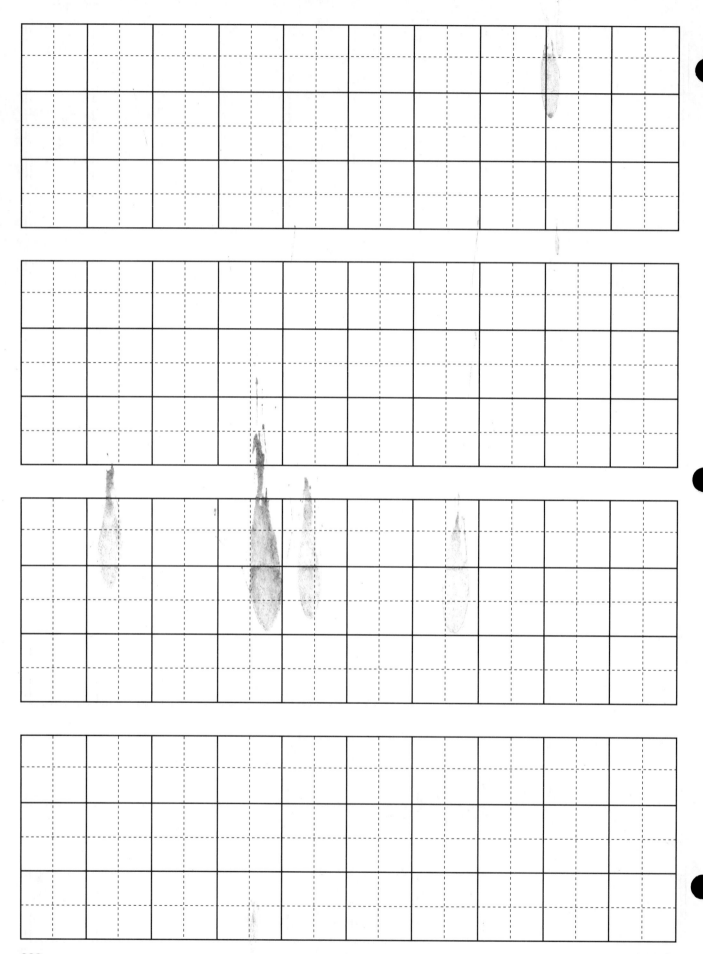

Name: _____ Date: _____

233

234

Name: _____ Date: _____

235

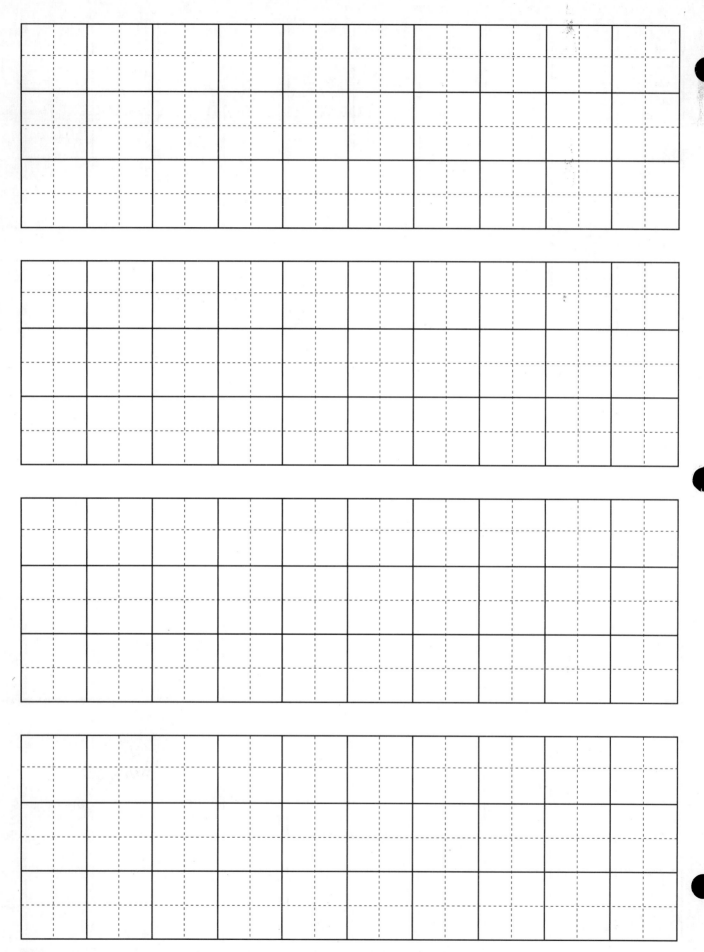